The

CHEAT

Code

The
CHEAT
Code

THE SECRET TWEAKS, HACKS & TIPS
TO GET NOTICED & GET AHEAD

Brian Wong

1 3 5 7 9 10 8 6 4 2

Virgin Books, an imprint of Ebury Publishing,
20 Vauxhall Bridge Road,
London SW1V 2SA

Virgin Books is part of the Penguin Random House group of companies
whose addresses can be found at global.penguinrandomhouse.com

Penguin
Random House
UK

First published in the United Kingdom by Virgin Books in 2016
First published in the United States by Crown Business in 2016

www.eburypublishing.co.uk

A CIP catalogue record for this book is available from the British Library

ISBN 9780753557242

Printed and bound in Great Britain by Clays Ltd, St Ives PLC

Penguin Random House is committed to a sustainable future for
our business, our readers and our planet. This book is made from
Forest Stewardship Council® certified paper.

MIX
Paper from
responsible sources
FSC
www.fsc.org   FSC® C018179

Dedicated to Mom, Dad, and Jason. I love you all very much, and it's because of you that everything here exists. Thank you.

Dedicated to the entire Kiip Family: all Kiipers, investors, customers, and partners. Thank you all for your amazing support. I'm excited for what the future holds.

CONTENTS

BE BALLSY

Learn how to get to the bolder version of yourself.

BE YOU

Remember: you are your greatest asset. Home in on your best skills and learn how to take them to the next level.

BE UNFORGETTABLE

Learn tips and tricks around PR, build your brand, and get attention for yourself and your ideas.

BE A TRAILBLAZER

Conventional wisdom is dead. There are better ways to get ahead—these cheats will put you in the right mind-set to be a leader among your peers and your industry.

THE CHEAT CODE

BE
BALLSY

LEARN HOW TO
GET TO THE BOLDER
VERSION OF YOURSELF.

APPRECIATE WHAT YOU'VE GOT—AND KILL YOUR FEAR!

TODAY IS AN INCREDIBLE TIME TO BE ALIVE. Opportunity is everywhere, and people have so much. There's never been a more level playing field, thanks to the Internet. Today anyone who can afford a cell phone has access to the Internet, and we all know that the Internet is crammed with knowledge, and that knowledge is power.

Access to knowledge is this century's revolution. Think about it. Back in the day, the expense of education was always a barrier to a better life, but now facts are free. If you don't know how to do something—literally anything, whether it's code or design a website, learn Mandarin, master the flute, or anything else— you can just go to the Internet and teach yourself or be taught by someone halfway around the world.

Today you don't even need a college education to be successful. Yes, college degrees are good, but today most employers care more about skills than degrees. On top of skills, smart employers care about drive, motivation, and *balls*—they're looking for skilled people with bold goals and ambitions, and the courage to go out and make them real. Sure, the world isn't perfect. And of course there are people with less access to opportunity than others. But in general, we are all surrounded by far more opportunities than ever before. It's impossible not to feel grateful.

So how did I come to develop such an optimistic view of the world? Here's the background. My dad grew up in a mud hut in China. His family struggled but was land-rich—certainly compared to everybody else. Then along came the communists, and suddenly successful people who'd created something of value were considered enemies of the state. So he escaped to Hong Kong in the bottom of a fishing boat when he was five years old and grew up penniless, but he felt lucky to have the chance for a good life.

That's how I felt too, growing up in Vancouver, British Columbia, far from the lap of luxury, hearing stories from my mother and father about how they didn't know that rice was white or tomatoes were red until shortly before they came to Canada as young adults—because they'd been too poor to afford anything but brown rice and too poor to be able to wait for a tomato to ripen before they ate it.

They were tireless and courageous, never took the easy way out, and succeeded professionally while raising a happy family. And now they appreciate every single thing they have.

So which came first: enough courage to create a life worthy of appreciation, or enough appreciation of life to have the daring that success demands?

I think attitude comes first. A positive attitude breeds success even more than success breeds a positive attitude—and in my opinion that's especially true when it comes to succeeding as an entrepreneur.

A law of behavioral psychology says that you can't be in a state of appreciation and a state of fear at the same time, and since the most successful of entrepreneurs are almost fearless, they must have the ability to appreciate what they've got, the ability to be grateful to be doing something interesting and fun.

When you're having fun, when you appreciate the things you have, you stop worrying about success and failure. This cool part of a Rudyard Kipling poem said it best: "If you can dream—and not make dreams your master; / If you can think—and not make thoughts your aim; / If you can meet with Triumph and Disaster / And treat those two impostors just the same . . . Yours is the Earth and everything that's in it, / And—which is more— you'll be a Man, my son!"

But, first, of course, you've got to have some balls. If you want to pursue your passions, you have to throw caution to the wind and take some risks.

I can speak from personal experience here. I came from an essentially unremarkable, middle-class background and had a business degree, but no fancy skills or credentials: no MBA, no specialized training in banking, advertising, or anything else.

But I have always been pretty fearless, which is why I had the initiative—at the ridiculously young age of nineteen—to jump into an industry that was gorged with incumbents, many of them huge, multinational advertising corporations, and many of whom had been in business since long before I was even born. And it's why I had the balls to propose an entirely new concept in advertising.

It came from a simple concept: People don't like ads. So why not create something they actually like?

Taking inspiration from the world of gaming, I thought what if, instead of just serving up annoying mobile ads that people would simply click away or ignore, we connected people with advertisers by offering them a free gift—like a moment of achievement in gaming when say, they leveled up or beat the boss? We later expanded that to other moments of achievement: for example, rewarding people serendipitously when they logged a run in their running app, or crossed off a to-do in their to-do list app. It was a radical concept, but what did I have to lose by trying to make it work? Nothing!

This fearlessness was the same attitude that drove my decision to skip four grades between kindergarten and high school and enroll in the University of British Columbia at age fourteen—a full four years ahead of my peers. Why did I do such a seemingly crazy thing? In the end, it all came back to fearless ambition. I felt ready to get out of school early and into the world and make things happen, rather than spend four more years sitting in a classroom—so I found a way to make that a reality. What did I have to lose then? Nothing! If it didn't work, I was just back where I started.

But it did work, and in a big way.

And along the way I discovered that success isn't about IQ. It's not about academic pedigree. It's not about who you know. It's not about the money you have behind you.

It's about you.

It's about you throwing caution to the wind, working your ass off, and having fun while you do it. It's about getting out there and acting like you've got nothing to lose.

Fuck fear. It's irrelevant, and it's the one great penalty that is completely self-imposed.

Steve Jobs once said: "Have the courage to follow your heart and intuition. They somehow already know what you truly want to become. Everything else is secondary."

So don't be afraid of what you can't do. Appreciate what

you've got—which is, by the way, more than most people have had since the dawn of civilization—and go from there. No matter what your dreams are, or what job or industry you're in, you've got an incredible opportunity at your fingertips. Let go of your fear, and instead reach for the stars.

GET IN OVER YOUR HEAD

THEY SAY THAT THE BEST WAY TO LEARN TO
swim is to jump into the deep end—as long as there's a life-
guard on duty, that is.

It's better than having somebody throw you in. Unfortunately, not everybody in the business world recognizes this. In
the days when soft-drink maker PepsiCo was a notoriously tough
company to work for, its unofficial motto was "There's no life-
guard at the Pepsi pool," with the corollary "What do they throw
you if you're drowning in the Pepsi pool? A rock." In other words,
the philosophy for how to succeed at many companies used to be
"sink or swim."

Most employers don't celebrate that gratuitously hard-ass
attitude these days, but the truth is that in today's competitive
landscape, if you don't jump in over your head every once in a
while, you'll probably be at a disadvantage, because whoever
hired you expects you to learn new things every day. At least you
hope they do, because the description of a job that carries no
challenge whatsoever is "dead end."

If you can do everything in your job without struggling, not only will you get stuck in your slot but you'll never flex your mind muscles, and pretty soon they'll start to atrophy.

This lesson came early for me, because I was four years younger than my brother, who's not only very smart but extremely likable, people-oriented, and much more extroverted than me. So to hang out with him, I had to stretch myself to act older than my age, learn from him and his friends, and show some maturity.

I learned the same lesson at about the same time at school, when I skipped a few grades. Going to class every day with kids several years older than me pushed me not just socially but mentally. I got to be very comfortable with the feeling of "What the hell is going on here?" because the answer was always "Whatever it is, it's pretty awesome, because I'm now learning things I didn't even know existed."

I became a member of the Fake It Till You Make It club, which is a Cheat in and of itself. It's a constant reminder: "Dude, you really are in over your head—whether you're fooling people or not—so keep your eyes open and your mouth (as best you can) shut, and just say yes to every opportunity you get." It'll be a constant learning experience, even if that means you sometimes have to flail around in the deep end.

You learn humility from that, and humility is the best possible trait for being in situations where you're in over your head. It's disarming and authentic, and so it will serve you just as well in the opposite situation. Even if you get to be a CEO, you'll still walk into a room with the attitude of "You guys are all so much smarter than me—that's why you're here, so I'll just toss out a couple of ideas." People love that. Who doesn't love respect? The best leaders don't just fake it till they make it; they fake it *after* they make it, but in the other direction.

For me, starting Kiip was a stretch, like jumping off a cliff and growing wings while you're falling—which is like entrepreneurship in general. I was not at that point an advertising professional, and I had no clue whether the idea I had—associating ads with rewards—would work, since at the time it didn't even exist.

We soon found ourselves playing ball with huge advertisers—like P&G, Unilever, and McDonald's—that were spending their money on mega-brands such as Apple's iAd and of course Google. But we jumped in with confidence. We said, "We've got a better way," and people took us seriously. Part of the cheat of jumping into the deep end is that people naturally assume you should be there, because you are.

Part of the reason we were confident was that we were letting our passion for our idea lead the way. We knew something was wrong in the whole universe of advertising (no one ever intentionally taps on banner ads on their mobile devices), and we wanted to fix it.

If you can find a universal problem, you can usually get universal buy-in to fix it. It's like if I say, "Oh, I'm going to fix traffic jams." There's not a human being in the world who would go, "Don't bother—I like getting stuck in traffic."

So I went into sales meetings with these major companies with a genuine belief in what we were doing, and it helped generate the major advertisers' initial buy-ins. I went in there with the total belief that our product could solve a problem they all had: Nobody wanted to click on their ads.

I could have gone in there intimidated, but why? When I jump in over my head, I *expect* to be challenged. That's why I do it.

If you jump in over your head, before you know it, you'll learn to swim.

Then you can jump in again, where the water's even deeper.

GO BALLS-TO-THE-WALL—BUT ONLY WHEN IT COUNTS

THE NUMBER-ONE THING I TOLD MYSELF BE-fore I started Kiip was, "I don't want to have any regrets. Ever." That's why I go balls-to-the-wall on all the important things I do. Of course, I can't completely control the outcome of everything, so sure, some things fail. But that's okay! In fact, if you're not failing on occasion, you're not aiming high enough.

When I fail after going all out, it doesn't feel like failure at all. It feels like an education. Regret comes only when you don't throw everything at your target. That's when you hear the ugly little voice saying, "What went wrong?"

Here's what went wrong: you.

You probably won't get a do-over either, because if you did a half-assed job on something, whoever gave you the opportunity to do it probably won't let you do it again. Or do anything else for them.

As I've said: Projects fail, people don't. More precisely, successful people don't, even when their projects don't pan out.

This begs a question: How does somebody live a 24/7 balls-to-the-wall lifestyle?

You don't. If you try to blast through life 24/7 like a rat in heat, you'll spontaneously combust so badly they'll need dental records to find out who you were.

I learned after my first couple of spontaneous combustions that I can't be this ridiculous guy who's on all the time, as everybody around me staggers to a halt and says, "Brian, how can you be so fucking energetic?" I learned (the hard way) that I can't afford to be that way. It's not sustainable.

Nobody is Superman. Not even Superman, because he's Clark Kent half the time. Think about it. If even Superman can't fire on all cylinders all the time, we mere mortals sure as hell can't.

Even so, people in high-rolling companies want their leaders to be superhuman, to be on all the time. They think it ignites everybody's confidence. That's human nature. Of course, to be a great leader you need to be able to stand up and kill it in an auditorium, or in a boardroom, or in your own office with your team. You've got to give a great performance—and not just an act, because there's a big difference between a performance and an act. A performance is when you're totally on top of your game, and an act is when you're pretending to be.

You need to, as I've said elsewhere, intentionally aim for excellence in moments that truly matter.

But then after your gig—and after the afterparty, and then after the after-afterparty, where the big things happen—you need to aim for moments of being a complete fucking sloth. A slacker. A slug. The kind of person who presses snooze—a couple of times, even—when the alarm goes off.

My record to date for the longest successful stretch of full-sloth behavior is thirty straight hours of sleep. It was after a U.S./ Asia crisscross trek where I bounced between the continents so fast I created my own time zone: Brian Daylight Time.

But that zone crumbled when I finally stopped moving. Thank God.

That's just Mother Nature's way of gently telling me: "Brian, honey, slow the fuck down, or I'll give you what God calls a near-death experience. Turn it off, if you ever want to turn it back on again."

So I did, and found to my surprise that after those first few minutes of sleep, I actually began to quite enjoy it.

The point is, it's important to give your all when it matters, but it's also very important to learn your limits. Honor them. Pay the piper. Feed the parking meter. Or do whatever cliché it takes to keep you ready to kill it when the right time comes. Then go beddy-bye to recharge your battery so you're ready to kill it again when the right opportunity comes along.

Don't be seduced by the saying "Die young and leave a beautiful corpse."

Make it "Die old and leave a beautiful corpse."

Because the truth is that *no one*, not even Superman, can go balls-to-the-wall all the time. Wouldn't you rather save your energy for those times when it really counts?

FIND THE ACTION

AT CERTAIN TIMES, IF YOU'RE LUCKY, YOUR OF-fice will be where the action is: the thinking, the deal making, and the getting things done. More often, though, the action will be somewhere else—and if you're really lucky, you'll have the kind of job that allows you to go there and find it.

Or you could just go there anyway, and *make* your job into that kind of job.

Last week started with a trip to see my family in Vancouver. Seeing family is as important as anything to me. Companies and co-workers come and go, but your family is forever, and if you forget that, you're nowhere, no matter where you are.

However, Vancouver was not exactly where the action was. So after spending some good quality time with my family, I took the red-eye to New York—sleeping on the plane, as usual, to show up feeling sharp—and hopped through a productive round of meetings all day. There's still not a city in the world that can beat New York for action. You can meet fifty of the most important one hundred people in advertising without walking more than twenty blocks, and just the sidewalks of that city have an energy of their own that seems to make action happen.

On Tuesday, I dived face-first into Internet Week in New York, which is like Fashion Week for Nerds. Instead of fashion shows, they have these big events, conferences, and parties for Internet advertisers. It has a real-time, come-as-you-are agenda that shifts radically from year to year, covering everything from topics such as programmatic ads to cross-channeling to disrupting traditional commercial patterns. Attendees even got to ring the opening bell on Wall Street. Talk about action.

Wednesday: new dawn, new destination. For most events, including Internet Week, you don't have to spend the full five days there. After twenty-four hours, it's usually been there, done that. The main thing is to go big, get noticed, and get going. If you create a splash with just one thing, people hear about it on social or traditional media, and it sends out concentric ripples of attention.

On Wednesday afternoon I had a speaking gig in Toronto, and the director of the event was freaking out, because I was cutting things close. So I busted out of New York and grabbed a flight that touched down in Toronto with time to spare—presuming the high-speed water taxi they provided was waiting and ready to rock.

It was. I jumped on and crashed through the waves with the wind in my hair—and if you're getting images of me shooting across the water toward my waiting limo like James Bond, I have to admit we're on the same wavelength right now.

I killed it at the Toronto speaking engagement, got a little media and Twitter coverage that started to spread outward, and made it back to New York in time for a private event for advertising CEOs. That event was pure essence of action. It didn't get coverage in the general media, but it did make waves with a smaller but better audience: better precisely because it *was* smaller, and exuded exclusivity and relevance to my industry.

By this time, people were already coming up to me and going, "Brian, I saw you on this or that the other day—it seems like you're everywhere!"

Then I jumped on another late-night flight back to San Francisco, with the time zones working in my favor, and was fresh for my appearance at Ad Tech, a great event that's exploded in recent years and is a hot nexus for global media, marketing, and tech. It covers stuff we need to know about now, like glanceable content, the future of phones as full-service virtual reality devices, and wearable tech, which was what my speech was about. More coverage. More concentric ripples of awareness.

Then back to Toronto. But this travelogue is getting a little insane—not quite on par with my actual life, but close enough—so I'll presume that my point has been made: Find the white-hot center of the action, play your part, and get gone!

When people think you're everywhere, they'll think you can do anything.

And when they start to think that, it starts to be possible.

PISS PEOPLE OFF

I'VE ALWAYS HAD AN ABILITY TO KNOW WHAT IRKS people, and lots of the time I just go ahead and do it. Why? Not to be a jerk, but because sometimes pissing people off is simply the best way to get your point across.

Of course, that doesn't mean you should say mean things or stupid things, like insulting somebody's race or gender, but if you passionately disagree with someone, it's best just to blurt it out and let the cards fall where they may.

A little shock value goes a long way in letting people know where you stand and that you care, and if you do it with a good heart it builds respect around you. You're the guy who says stuff other people won't. It can even make you lovable. Comedians have known that forever.

The cheat becomes even more effective when you add a spoiler. By that I mean you sort of announce that you're going to piss somebody off by saying something like, "No offense, but . . ." or "You may not want to hear this, but . . . ," then come out with the zinger. What can they do? If they get pissed, then they're the asshole, because hey, you warned them. And if they're an asshole, you probably don't want to do business with them anyway, so you might as well say what's on your mind.

All you've got to do is make it clear you're passionate about what you think, and that you're saying it because you think it's something somebody should hear. When people see how much I care about making advertising a choice instead of an invasion, I can get away with all kinds of critical remarks. People mostly remember that I'm sincere about giving them something of value, and they forgive me for saying all kinds of things they wouldn't overlook if I was just some dude with a chip on his shoulder.

The same thing carries over to brands. Apple, for example, is known to be a very passionate and authentic brand, so when they piss people off by making a mistake, people forgive them. If a company perceived as just being interested in taking your money, on the other hand, makes a mistake, they get crucified—because there's no emotional connection to them.

You might recall how a few years ago Apple made a major screw-up with the antennas of their iPhone 4, and it kicked off a global tidal wave of complaints. To make matters worse, they didn't even acknowledge the glitch for a few weeks, and it came after a bunch of other problems with the new iOS.

For some brands, this would have been a death sentence, but not for Apple. Instead, people were like, "No worries. It's cool, we know you'll sort it out."

Why was the public so forgiving? Partly because everybody was still in love with the legacy of Steve Jobs, who was never the world's most diplomatic guy (in fact, he may have invented Cheat 5 about pissing people off) but was somebody who never got accused of not giving a shit. People knew he lived and breathed his products, and in a world of depersonalized, manipulative commerce, that was exactly what it took to build brand loyalty, and in turn create the most golden of opportunities: the second chance. When you get a do-over on your screw-ups, you can almost always find the fix.

All of this is part of the cheat of tying your business to a grand concept that will serve the greater good—the kind of thing Elon Musk does.

It all starts with loving your idea and the business you build from it, and getting the idea in the first place because you love people and want to make your money doing something that's good for them. On the other hand, if you're just out for power or greed or to prop up a shaky ego and think you can get away with a mess-up by means of a quick "My bad"—good luck. So before you ask someone for a second chance, make sure you deserve it. If you put yourself in a position to deserve forgiveness, however, you'll be amazed at how easy it can be to get away with speaking your mind or voicing an unpopular position—even when it means pissing people off.

SMELL THEIR FEAR

I'M ALWAYS HONEST IN BUSINESS, AND I'M ALWAYS fair—not just because it's the right thing to do, but because it creates success. But there's never a day I don't want to win. And there's never a day when somebody isn't trying to make me lose.

Business is competition. That's a universal and eternal truth.

It's been said that the art of business often resembles the art of war, and that's absolutely true. That may sound brutal on the surface, but there's actually a Darwinian beauty to it. More often than not, in the battle for market share, only the strong survive, and only the good products sell. Over time this benefits not just companies but consumers too. Fortunately, capitalism is still mostly a meritocracy.

The Cheat Code is filled with ways to get a leg up on your competition, but here's a cheat geared specifically toward winning your most hard-fought battles: Know what your opponent fears most. That's generally their primary point of vulnerability, and, in turn, your primary point of opportunity.

Smelling the fear of your competitors is a difficult art, because people are good at concealing their weaknesses. So to win at this game you've got to learn how to read people as they really are, rather than as the personalities they project.

Unfortunately, our digital world makes it even easier for your competitors to hide their fears and flaws. When you use a text or email to provoke a direct competitor into revealing their hidden vulnerabilities, you never really know how they reacted to it. You rarely get an immediate response to a provocative email, because people will take time to think it over. As a result, you just get a carefully considered response (sometimes crafted and vetted by their publicist), often with nothing more revealing than an emoticon. This is just one more reason to always deal with people as directly as possible: face-to-face, or via Skype, or at least on the phone. A lot of people are afraid to do that because it makes them uncomfortable. But remember, success is most often found far from your comfort zone. If it wasn't, more people would be successful.

So suck it up. Go on Skype, or hop on a plane, and get some personal, direct contact with the people who are blocking your goals.

People say, "Keep your friends close, but your enemies closer." That's because when your enemies are close, it's much easier to find their weak spot. And believe me, they have one, no matter how successful they are or how confident they seem on the surface. Everyone on the planet has one or two things that they're insecure about.

The moment you find that chink in their armor, you begin to learn a lot about them and what drives them.

You get a better sense of why they make certain decisions, including the ones that are interfering with your goals.

If their insecurity is, say, that they've never held on to a major client for more than a year, it might mean that they're now trying to do something that creates loyalty and sustainability. Or it could mean the opposite: that they're inherently afraid to commit and unable to change. No matter what it is, you've got something to think about, as the puzzle pieces of their behavior begin to form a pattern that ultimately reveals what they want most, how they plan to get it, and what they'll do next.

The shortcut to their vulnerability is information. Try to get a feel for them, and then ask a hot-button question that sounds specific but is really pretty general, like, "Was business slow last year?" or "Are you having a hard time holding on to good talent right now?" Those things are true of at least half of all people, but if it's really a sore spot for them, they'll feel like you're reading their mind. It may ruffle feathers (see Cheat 5 on pissing people off), but it is a way to instantly understand someone on a potentially deeper level.

If they just give you a straight, simple answer, it usually means it's not a big issue for them. If so, drop it, and look for something else. But if they're evasive or, at the other extreme, start giving you too much information, it tends to indicate they're touchy about it.

Touchy is good. It usually leads to the disclosure of other insecurities, since fears tend to cluster in certain areas. Insecurity about the lack of a college degree, for example, might be coupled with insecurity about intelligence or drive, and so on.

As you learn what makes people tick, you know how to predict what to expect from them, defend yourself against them, and ultimately beat them.

You absolutely do not do this to gratuitously hurt anybody, and you absolutely shouldn't take it so far that you turn into an asshole. Once you know where their fear is, you don't *need* to be an asshole. You can be kind and gentle, or you can just stop engaging. You know what you need to know.

Your smartest competitors have probably been doing that to you for some time. They have no ill will. They just want to win.

You should feel flattered. Winning feels best when you defeat a worthy opponent.

Not only that, when *they* figure out your fears, it motivates you to do one of the most important things in life: conquer them.

If you're the only fearless person in a room, it's almost like an automatic win. So go ahead and celebrate. You've earned it.

DON'T ASK—ANNOUNCE!

ONE OF THE GREAT JEDI MIND TRICKS OF business—and almost any situation—is to tell people you're going to do something before you do it. Don't ask their permission; just tell them. Then do it.

If you do it right, it has a weird way of seeming considerate, but also confident and authoritative at the same time.

The very act of announcing something confidently somehow endows it with legitimacy and validity. People usually just assume that because you've thought it over, it's probably a brilliant idea, or at least they become deferential to your intent. It's wild! It's a cheat I use all the time.

It's way more effective than just doing something without announcing it first. Surprises are what piss people off. They think you don't care about their opinion, and for all they know, it's something you just pulled out of your ass, without thinking.

I learned this through Kiip's board meetings, where I'm dealing with some of the smartest people in business. These people hate surprises. Why shouldn't they? Nobody likes to have something shoved down their throat without having a chance to consider it. So I try to talk to every one of them before the meeting, over the phone or over coffee, and run through the agenda, so that when game time comes, they aren't caught off guard.

I do it deferentially because these people deserve respect, but note that I'm not asking for their approval. If they have good input, I listen. But I'm not asking for permission; I'm telling.

As a result, the board meeting is literally me repeating what I already told everybody separately, and that's okay. Everybody feels in the loop, and the meeting is smooth. People have ideas and I consider them, but there's never any drama, because everybody knows what's coming.

The golden rule of Kiip board meetings is: no surprises.

I carried this cheat over to meetings with my own team. They all get the agenda before the meeting, so everybody's comfortable with it and feels like we've got a good plan. If somebody has ideas to make the plan even better, great!

Try it out. You don't need to be a CEO to use this cheat. You can use it with your colleagues, with your clients, even in your everyday life. Next time a line in Starbucks feels like it's turning into a fossil, just move forward and say, "Excuse me, I'm just gonna grab something and get out of your way"—and do it. What can they do? Call the hall monitor? People are understanding if you give them reason to be.

Or when you're crowded into an airplane ramp and need to make a call that distracts other people, say to somebody loud enough for others to hear, "Sorry, I've gotta hop on the phone for a second." Your small rudeness becomes politeness, and nobody's shooting eye daggers your way.

When I give speeches, the event coordinator usually says something along the lines of "Don't go up there and pitch your company." I'm always like, "Well, I'm planning to talk a bit about my company and what I do, since that's why I'm here, and then I'll talk about other stuff." They know it's too late for me to change my speech. That ship has sailed. So I give the speech I came with, making sure I do a good job, and the coordinator is happy—way happier than if I hadn't warned him I was going to mention my company.

When you tell people what you're going to do before you do it, they won't be surprised when you do it. And nobody likes surprises. You'll get a better outcome every time.

THINK ON YOUR FEET!

ONE OF MY MOST VALUABLE ASSETS IN BUSI-
ness is my ability to feel very comfortable and confident in
front of an audience. That's essential for success, because no matter what business you're in, audiences are everywhere, from the
main stage at Cannes Lions or SXSW (or the equivalent for your
industry) to a boardroom where you're pitching clients or having
a meeting with your own team.

I had no idea when I first developed this ability that it would
someday be important. That happens all the time: New skills
seem trivial. In reality, no skills are trivial.

I never set out to learn how to be a good business speaker. I
learned it inadvertently, by taking a number of speech arts classes
in school. That's where I got accustomed to performing and
thinking on my feet. It's one of those things that is scary at first
(surveys show that public speaking is the most common of all
phobias) but ends up being fun and extraordinarily rewarding.
(Bonus cheat: Master something that most people fear.)

An even better training ground for public speaking, I've
found, is a background in improvisational acting or comedy, even
if it's just in a college class. Over time, I noticed that almost all

the great salespeople I hired had done at least a little improv at some point. Now that's one of the things I look for when I hire. It seems to make all the difference.

When you put somebody with improv skills in a sales meeting, you can see those skills come out. They're animated, interactive, charismatic, and clever, and they clearly come up with things on the spot. It's insane to watch some of these guys pitch.

I seriously believe that acting or performing gives you a better grasp on how to act in the moment and how to express yourself in all kinds of situations, both in business and outside of it. It turns the action of persuasion into an art, and the act of communication into a seamless dance.

Ultimately, all drama, whether it's onstage or in a business meeting, is about communication—communication so attuned that it moves others toward your perceptions and beliefs. In other words, communication is central to the art of getting people to buy in.

Whether in the boardroom or the comedy cellar, performing starts with reading your audience and getting so far into their heads that, ideally, you feel like you're them and they feel like they're you. Once you've captured their wavelength, the rest is gravy. Stated most simply: You put yourself in their shoes.

Once you feel like you really know whom you're talking to, you need to carry your message to people—or carry people to your message—by evoking powerful feelings and emotions, like surprise, happiness, trust, and hope. You need to know when to pause, whom to look at (and whom not to look at), what words to stress, how to make eye contact, how to fake eye contact, and when to shut the hell up.

Most important of all, you need to know how to *evoke*. The end game of acting is not to show the audience the emotion that you feel, but to subtly bring *them* to feel it.

There are lots of ways to do that, such as by underacting or by using body language that triggers feelings subliminally. That prompts the audience to, in effect, fill in the blanks with their own hopes and dreams.

A central principle of acting is: Let the audience do the acting.

Get up there, win their hearts and minds, and then step back and let them do the rest of the work. When somebody tells you, "Your product is so good it sold itself," just smile, agree with them, take a bow, and get off the stage.

Then go back out and do it again and again. The show must go on, and when it does, the role starts to feel so real that it's not even acting.

SCREW THE MBA

IN MY OPINION, THE SIX HOTTEST SCHOOLS FOR entrepreneurship are, in order of excellence:

1. Wharton School at the University of Pennsylvania
2. Harvard Business School
3. Foster School of Business at the University of Washington
4. Whitman School of Management at Syracuse University
5. Booth School of Business at the University of Chicago
6. The School of Rock

I'm fucking with you. But you probably didn't know until you hit the School of Rock. That's how brainwashed so many of us can be.

Now that I've pissed off everybody who's connected with all of the above—except maybe Jack Black—please allow me to piss people off even further by saying that for the most part, an MBA is a colossal waste of money.

I think college is an excellent investment for a business career, but entrepreneurship—as a specific realm of business—is extremely hard to teach, much like the performing arts or high-level athletics. Sure, a certain amount of teaching helps, but in general either you have the X-factor for those things or you don't.

College and MBA programs in entrepreneurship are the hot new thing now simply because of demand, not because of their proven value. As long as students want to pay exorbitant tuitions to be taught to be entrepreneurs, schools will be willing to take their money.

But the reality is that one of the best educations for an entrepreneur is just learning the basics of business—economics, finance, accounting, marketing, human resources, organizational behavior—and a few other skills, along with a healthy dose of arts and sciences.

Even a basic business education, though, can produce mixed results. The problem is that business school education is optimized to produce cookie-cutter grads, because that's what the big companies want. A school's incentive in the greater scheme of commerce is to be a factory for accountants and other standard business professions. They pump students in and pump them out, and then the big companies hire these kids for a dime, sell their services for a dollar, and everybody feels like a winner—except for the students-turned-bankers, who end up $100,000 in debt and never get a chance to figure out who they *really* are or want to be.

A lot of eighteen- and nineteen-year-olds decide to study business because they think, "Well, I don't really know what I want to be when I grow up, but I'll choose finance, because I'm going to graduate and make $100,000 as a banker. Then at least I can implement the banker's 2/4/2 System of Success: Borrow money at 2 percent, loan it at 4 percent, and be on the golf course by 2:00 p.m."

Even before these kids can legally buy beer, they quit being themselves—which is a messed-up way to wander through life (unless you were born to bank—or play golf).

My advice is to study what you love at a school you can afford. True, a top-notch school might force you to work your balls off. But as discussed in Cheat 1, in today's world of limitless free information, you can also force yourself to learn your balls off—without paying $45,000 a year in tuition.

You just need to commit to learning to be great at something, and pay close attention to exactly what it takes to make money from your mad skills.

If you think business school is the right fit for you, then go for it. Just don't think that you can enroll in a curriculum that will make you the new Elon Musk or Steve Jobs or Sergey Brin or Larry Page, because those jobs are taken. Learn to be you.

If you're good at it, you can monetize it. If you're excellent at it, then you already are, in a very real sense, an entrepreneur. By that I mean you're the world's first you. Get good enough at that, and people will line up at your door, whether or not you have a fancy MBA.

DON'T TREAT PEOPLE WITH MONEY AND POWER LIKE GOD

THE FOUNDERS OF START-UPS OFTEN MAKE THE mistake of fearing rejection from investors, as if the investors hold the keys to the kingdom.

But the people who invest in you are just people, and the sooner you realize that, the better your life will be.

Think of investors like this: They are people with the money.

Think of yourself as this: You are the person with the idea.

If that isn't a fair and equal exchange, there wouldn't be any exchange at all.

When somebody invests money in you, they don't do it to make you rich. They do it to make themselves rich. Why else would they do it?

If you know that, you won't bend over backward and take a beating during either the negotiation phase or the operational phase.

During the negotiation phase with investors, you don't go into any meeting thinking that this is the be-all and end-all. You go in thinking that these are just a few of the people who are lining up to give you money. That's not arrogance. That's reality.

Lack of reality comes from your own fear that you're not worth the money. If you're really not worth it, though, you shouldn't be in that meeting. Wait until you are worth it, and then come back. Or just wait until your fear subsides enough for you to see that you are worth it.

Everybody has some green in their pocket these days, so it's not like one rejection is going to kill you or your business. If one of the investors you meet doesn't want to make a deal, you've still got a thousand more investors to meet.

In fact, you almost never convince the first potential investor you talk to. I lucked out with my first venture capitalist (see Cheat 53), but that was extremely unusual. I've been turned down by many other investors since then. I just closed an incredible deal with an investor, but before that, about forty others rejected the same offer.

Being turned down is not the end of the world, unless you make it feel like that. In fact, rejection can often be a good thing; it not only helps you build resilience and grow a thicker skin but also often comes with information that can help you improve your pitch.

Another important thing to remember about your investor is that he's not really risking his own money from his own pocket. No matter what trappings of wealth he might display, the person you're talking to is rarely the one who makes the ultimate decision. He might not even be working directly for the person who makes the decision.

Kiip, at this time, has been involved with seven venture capitalists. Each one of them is part of a fund that holds hundreds of millions of dollars, and none of that money is theirs. They are the investment managers.

Some funds are even larger, in the billions of dollars. These funds aggregate the wealth of a vast number of people and include huge holdings such as pension funds.

The funds manage these enormous amounts of money in an extraordinarily macrocosmic manner. They're like, "Let's give this company $50 million so that we can check off a venture capital box, diversify our investments, and make sure that we keep our internal rate of return at the level we want it to be this fiscal year. Or maybe $75 million."

The person you talk to has partners—probably a number of them—and has to talk to those partners. Ultimately somebody reports to a limited partner, who makes the decision.

That doesn't mean that the venture capitalist you talk to isn't brilliant, or doesn't have great responsibilities and authority. It just means he's not your Warren Buffett. He's playing with somebody else's money. Just like you.

That doesn't make it less serious. Just less scary. It also makes his rejection more endurable.

A similar *Cheat Code* principle to make rejection not sting so much is this: Realize that nobody gives a shit about you. In short, a turndown is nothing personal.

If they actually did care about you, that would really suck.

This is true for any rejection you might receive from any powerful business person, whether from an investor, a potential client, or a boss. It isn't personal, and they aren't God.

So after a rejection, just go back to your office with a smile on your face, set up more appointments, and remind yourself that your project really is the shit, no matter how that investor saw it. After all, if everybody could see everything, nobody could get rich.

So don't worry when you get rejected. You're not alone. It's happened before and it'll happen again. These are just people— it's not the word of God.

GET HIGH-POWERED PEOPLE'S PHONE NUMBERS

Y OU'LL EITHER LOVE THIS CHEAT OR HATE IT.
You'll think it alone is worth the price of the book—or you'll think it's so obvious that it shouldn't even be in the book.

I am of the opinion that the first attitude is correct, because I once had no idea this cheat was possible, and now I use it all the time.

It's a cheat you can do anytime you're in physical proximity to any high-level executive whom you'd like to be able to reach at will but who's surrounded by layers of people who screen calls, emails, texts, and anything else that might be a distraction. You ask for the number.

I do it at all the conferences I go to, like South by Southwest and the Consumer Electronics Show. You just go up to somebody, introduce yourself, shake hands, chat for a bit, and get to know each other. Then you get around to talking about their event or their party. They tell you that they can make sure that you can get in even with the line outside. Then you say, "What's the best way to reach you?"

They hardly ever give you the number of their call screener or gatekeeper, because they don't know it. They usually just say,

"Call me or text me at such-and-such number." It's the only one they know: their own. They'll usually suggest their phone number because it'll be the most convenient way in the moment.

Why shouldn't they share their number? They can see you're harmless, it would be rude to just blow you off, and it's the easiest thing to do.

That's it. The whole cheat. Easy, right?

Larger lesson: Whatever you're trying to do, try the easy way first.

NEVER LEARN THE RULES

THE SCARIEST PERSON AT A POKER TABLE FULL of veterans is not the man in the cowboy hat, the guy wearing sunglasses at night, or the guy in the tuxedo who's casually stirring a martini with one hand and riffling through his chips with the other.

The scariest person is the one who doesn't know the rules of poker as well as the others.

If you've read all the books about poker, watched all the online tutorials, and heeded all the expert advice, and then you sit down to play poker with the pros—you're going to get wrecked. Because the pros know the rules and conventional actions and reactions better than you ever will, and they know what you're going to do. When you follow their rules and play their game, the odds are stacked as high as a mountain.

But if you sit down at that poker table blissfully unaware of the rules, you're going to terrify those veterans. They can't read you. They can't calculate your actions. You're bringing something new to the table, and they don't know what it is. Maybe it's crazy, maybe it's dangerous, or maybe it's the future.

Business—especially tech—is a lot like a poker game. There

are some seriously talented individuals at the table who spend all day hearing amazing ideas from brilliant people. They are veterans of the pitch. If it seems like they've heard everything, or feels like they're constantly calculating, it's because they have, and are. They know the odds backward and forward.

You walk into a room full of these individuals, and you immediately think: "What can they possibly want from me?"

They know what looks good and sounds good in a presentation, and they know what they want to hear and what they want to see. Their preferences—and their rules of thumb for doing business—start to look identical. It makes their job easier.

But it doesn't make your job easier. That's exactly how they want it.

So the cheat is: Don't go in there and play by their rules. Don't even study their rules.

The scariest guy at a table of business sharks is someone like me—a guy who's created a different way to play the game. It was especially like that when I was nineteen and had just started my company—because back then I didn't know anything. All I knew was that I wanted to win.

When I was nineteen, first pitching potential investors about my company, I had no idea what I was doing. I figured I should probably have a mock-up, or at least something to show people, so I wouldn't look like some kid with a great idea and nothing to illustrate it. But due to my lack of experience, my "mock-up" consisted of a few slides I put together using my existing knowledge of HTML.

It was far from a slick presentation, but it got people's attention, and they saw that I had the balls to do things my way instead of the old way. They also saw that I simply wanted to *do*.

Since I wasn't obsessing over dotting *i*'s and crossing *t*'s, my passion for the product came out. I looked like a kid who was really, really passionate about his idea—which was a damn good idea—but who didn't know everything in the world yet, and didn't pretend to. That was the key.

To veterans at a poker table, that's terrifying.

To investors and executives, that's electrifying.

ASK YOURSELF: WHAT'S THE WORST THING THAT CAN HAPPEN?

THERE'S A SIMPLE CHEAT THAT CAN DISABLE fear: Contemplate the worst-case scenario—within reason—and go from there.

More often than not, the worst thing that can happen isn't particularly devastating. Sure, it might be a setback, or even the end of something you love, but it's not the end of the world.

If you perceive big problems unreasonably, as if your life is over, you're probably not going to make it as an entrepreneur. If so, you may be wise to find another avenue for your ambitions.

When you look for absolute, life-shattering catastrophe in every problem, you usually find it.

This phenomenon extends far beyond business. If you think breaking up with your girlfriend or boyfriend means you'll never be in love again, you're just creating a self-fulfilling prophecy. When something like that happens, the smart thing to do is take a deep breath—literally and figuratively—assess your damages, and realize that what happened is endurable.

Things could be worse.

Are there other fish in the sea? You bet! A whole ocean of them!

Not succeeding happens to everybody—all the time. Almost all entrepreneurs, and most people in general, have at least as many failures as successes. Thomas Edison once described himself as the man who created a thousand ways not to invent the lightbulb. He wasn't just being humble. He was proud that he had the strength of character and the breadth of intellect to deal with that much failure.

He did not have a thousand excuses for not inventing the lightbulb. He had no interest in, nor need for, excuses.

He had reasons, though. And each reason was something that ruled out an ineffective method and brought him closer to one that worked.

The mere fact that you make excuses—whether they're valid or not—means you are not naturally entrepreneurial. It means that you have discovered a way to demotivate yourself. The ability to demotivate yourself is enough, in and of itself, to rule you out as an entrepreneur.

The exercise for moving beyond the haunting fear of disaster is simple. Ask yourself, "What's the worst thing that can happen if this doesn't work?"

An entrepreneurial person realizes that the worst thing that might happen is virtually never something that cannot be endured.

Sure, you might lose a contract, a job, your company, your house, your life savings, or the esteem of others. That would suck. But life would go on.

Some people can accept the continuation of life as *enough*.

Some people can't.

If you can't, you are not entrepreneurial.

In fact, not charging forward in the face of loss and fear sets you up to suffer in a multitude of ways: financially, romantically, socially, and psychologically.

When things go south, look for something else to do. When you find it, ask yourself what's the worst-case scenario if you proceed.

Then proceed, with gusto!

BE
YOU

REMEMBER: YOU ARE YOUR
GREATEST ASSET. HOME IN
ON YOUR BEST SKILLS AND
LEARN HOW TO TAKE THEM
TO THE NEXT LEVEL.

DON'T PITCH YOUR BUSINESS— PITCH YOURSELF!

THERE I WAS AT SOUTH BY SOUTHWEST, THE Oscars of emerging technology and start-ups, and my voice sounded like a cross between a talking rooster's and a motivational speaker's, because in the last fifty hours I'd met about five hundred new people out of the fifty-one thousand who were there—and they were some of the most interesting people on earth. They were the future of business, and that made them part of my future. SXSW is the quintessential networking event for entrepreneurs who want to lead change instead of follow it.

Think of SXSW as Davos for Nerds.

Imagine all the primary players from thousands of the hottest start-ups crammed together in one big room at an insane, high-octane event. This is not the time to spare your throat. It's the time for ABP: Always Be Pitching. But the key to making the most out of an opportunity like SXSW is not to be pitching your business; it's to be pitching your own personal brand.

People working for a company tend to think of that company as their brand. That's why it's good to work for a big brand, like Google. You introduce yourself this way: "Hi, I'm John Smith, of

Google." People are like: "Mr. Google, it's such a thrill to meet you. I've heard so much about you!"

Your company is rarely your primary brand, though. Your main brand is you. Don't forget that, and don't be ashamed of it. Everybody loves being on a team—especially an all-star one like Google—but think about it this way: People change teams (and jobs) all the time, and you'll still be *you* long after you've left Google.

One variation, therefore, of ABP is Always Be Pitching Yourself.

If you look around, you'll see that the smart people at high-opportunity networking events like these are pitching their own persona—their selfhood. They're making connections, not deals. They know that deals are for later, if ever.

There's scattered talk about who's doing what, which companies are being funded for how much, and so on. But the *real* conversations are always about the same two topics: you and the person you're talking to.

In other words, your goal should be to get people to invest in *you,* not your project—because smart people never invest their time, money, or reputation in just a project. It's always personal.

Plus, when you open yourself up and let people see who you are—as a person, not just the extension or representation of the company you work for—you're more open to the serendipity of meeting the right people: That's how I met Pete Cashmore, CEO of Mashable, a few years ago at SXSW. I went to the Mashable party and a mutual friend just said, "Pete, meet Brian, and Brian, this is Pete." Very casual. No expectations. Neither of us knew much about the other, but we found out we were both starting new companies, and that's something that's easy to bond over.

Back then neither Pete nor I thought we'd soon be on *Forbes*'s "30 Under 30," a list of the most prominent young people in business, or that Pete would be one of *Time*'s "100 Most Influential People of 2012." Our meeting wasn't about where we were going or how one of us might be able to help the other out in the future. It was about two guys with similar interests getting to know each other a little.

Think how different a relationship like that is from one that starts with somebody giving you an elevator pitch along the lines of, "I've got an amazing business idea: Uber for pizza! Boom!" That relationship is just about that one idea, and when the idea dies, the relationship goes with it.

Also, the reality is, nobody gives a fuck about what you're doing, or your funding, or the last deal you closed. Why should they? You're just one of a million start-ups at a place like SXSW.

That is, nobody gives a fuck about you until you help them understand why they should: because of who you are as a human being. In other words, if you want to make a true connection, you need to cut through the superficial clutter of deals, titles, and achievements (news flash: people will see right through them) and show your true self.

So you don't go to a place like SXSW—or any gathering of important people for whatever industry or line of work you're in—full of hubris. You go in grateful: to be at this place, to be learning and growing, and to be making extraordinary friends.

That creates the serendipity of right person, right place, right time, and those are the connections that eventually bring opportunities that lead to your success.

But the key word here is "eventually." I rarely do business right away with the people I meet. Instead, I wait for the right time and the right opportunity—and in the meantime, I continue to cultivate the relationship, keep it strong. I still haven't done any business with Pete Cashmore—but maybe someday I will.

The point is, over time, authentic relationships will yield

value for your business, in addition to the value they yield for your life as friendships. It might start when you see the other person again at a conference, at a party, or at some other industry event. Then you'll meet as old friends, who know each other for the right reason—that you like and respect each other—rather than the wrong reason, which is that you think you can make money off each other.

The truly golden relationships start when your goal is to not force anything but to share some of yourself with people, learn from them.

I've found that if you ask people for advice, they'll give you money, and that if you ask them for money, they'll give you advice. But the higher you climb in business, the less your relationships revolve around money and the more they revolve around being the person other people want to spend time with.

It's really fun to be the guy people want to be around. I experienced this a couple of years ago at SXSW, when Kiip threw an incredible party cosponsored by a client, Decentralized Dance Party. DDP coordinates sensational events all around the world—the kind of parties that stick in your mind forever and are well worth the expense. After all, nothing amortizes better than a good memory.

Our DDP party in Austin consisted of taking an FM radio tuner off an iPod, synching it to two hundred boomboxes, and turning it into a huge parade that marched all around the city. It was sick—everybody was talking about it. At least a thousand people got involved, and when people found out that Kiip was behind the event, nobody needed to ask me, "What does your company do?"

Everybody just wanted to know the guy leading the parade.

LIGHT YOUR HALO!

M Y FIRST DAY AT COLLEGE, I HAD A HARD choice to make. I was fourteen, younger than just about anybody else at the University of British Columbia, and needed to decide how to present myself. I could be seen either as the young, insecure, introverted kid who was lucky to be there, or the young, confident, extroverted kid who was lucky to be there.

Problem: on the Myers-Briggs Type Indicator, I'm 55 percent extroverted and 45 percent introverted. I tell people I'm an introverted extrovert (and a shocking number say, "Me too!").

But I knew even then that the first impression you create in any setting sets the tone for the rest of the time you're there—especially if it's negative. If you start out like a hermit or a grouch, it's hard to reverse that.

But, Myers-Briggs aside, my choice back then sort of made itself, because I was just so excited to meet these people. I'd always been around bright kids—and older kids too, because I'd sailed through school—but the UBC students were smart and interesting on a whole new level, especially in the business program, my major.

So I put a big smile on my face—really, it was more like I couldn't get it off—and started saying hi to everybody I saw.

I can't overemphasize the power of a smile! It can disarm someone who's angry, warm up someone who doesn't know why they're talking to you, make an awkward situation funny, and make a stranger a friend.

It's like putting the sun on your face. It lights you up, and that light shines on the person you're smiling at. Key lesson: A good impression isn't about how you make people feel about you, it's how you make them feel about themselves.

Sometimes after I've talked to somebody, I forget what we talked about, but I always remember how I felt. If people remember feeling happy around you and laughing, that's the best impression ever.

A smile helps create what's called the *halo effect,* the element of a first impression that makes people look for reasons to like you instead of reasons to be wary of you. And when people like you, it opens doors.

You can say the exact same words to somebody with a smile on your face—or without one, and get a totally different response.

There's even a theory from psychology that says smiling makes you happy almost as much as happiness makes you smile.

At UBC, my halo effect made me super-popular despite my age. It even helped get me elected to a student office—without most people knowing what I stood for.

The halo effect can be equally effective in business. At the first company I worked for—Digg, a news aggregator—I did the same ultra-friendly meet-and-greet, and it had the same magical effect.

Think about it: Isn't that how you make decisions about other people? If somebody is nice to you, you tend to trust them. And in turn you don't give them the third degree. You give them opportunities instead.

These days, a good reputation starts with what other people say when your name comes up. It's like: "Brian, yeah, I know him—he's a cool guy. He's always wearing a smile."

You might wonder what the hell "cool guy" means. It means whatever the listener wants it to mean. (Huge cheat coming up: *People are looking for reasons to like you.*) If somebody hears that you're a cool guy, they'll fill in the blanks with whatever they want it to mean: a loyal guy, a smart guy, a nice guy, a fun guy.

Each time your name gets mentioned, your halo gets brighter and brighter. As your reputation expands, people keep hearing the same good things about you. Your halo turns into a force field and keeps negative bullshit at bay.

The best part is that you've already got your halo right on your face. So light it up, light up the people around you—and get ready for good things to happen!

KNOW YOUR SUPERPOWER!

HERE'S ANOTHER THING I LEARNED FROM EN-
tering the business world at a ridiculously young age:
No matter who you are or what you do in life, you have a
superpower—and by that I mean something you do far better
than most people. If you're not using it, you're crazy.

If I ever interview you for a job, expect me to ask: "What's
your superpower?"

Here's mine: I'm really good at getting people excited about
stuff. That's my job, and I love it. Or: I love it, and that's my job.
Both are equally true.

I can sit in front of you and make you excited about whatever—
just by how I describe it and how I feel. It's contagious, and you'll
just go, "Wow! That is so cool!"

I do it even when I don't *need* to. Can't help it. That's just me.
And that's how I know it's my superpower.

So what's yours?

You probably already know what it is. If you're hesitating,
it's probably just because we live in an era of fake humility and
you don't want to look arrogant. But confident people aren't arrogant. They don't need to be.

Don't be afraid to know your superpower and name it. Nobody will mind. We're all looking for all the help we can get.

I learned my first superpower from my mother, when I was a kid playing hockey. My mom took me to practice, stuck around and watched, and helped me see my strengths and weaknesses. She taught me to hone my strengths into veritable superpowers, and how to play away from my weaknesses.

In the early years, I could compete with almost anybody, but then all the guys started getting big and muscular, and I stayed average in size. My mom said, "That's your new strength. Speed. Agility. Wits."

It wasn't the mainstream style, but it kept me in the game and taught me a huge life lesson: Don't try to fix your weaknesses. Build your strengths—and make one into a superpower.

This lesson has served me well time and time again. Long before I quit hockey, I looked around for other things I loved and was good at, and realized I was good with computers and had an eye for design. So I downloaded a program on graphic design and taught it to myself in no time.

Remember, we're in the golden age of do-it-yourself learning. You don't need a certificate or degree to actually know something—just a little aptitude and the willingness to give something a try.

So I got pretty good at design, but my design work never got perfect. Yet I kept trying. Big mistake. I did quite a bit of the design in my first two companies, and I started to feel good about my skills—until I met one of my current partners, Amadeus Demarzi, an interaction designer who worked at a hot design agency called Sequence. Amadeus blew me away. Design was his superpower. That's when I realized it wasn't mine. So I told him, "You do the design stuff, and I'll build the business side of the company."

This was an easy decision and turned out to be one of the best I ever made. Moral of the story: When you divide tasks according to strengths, amazing things happen—fast.

It's fine not to be good at everything. People who have mad talents at one thing usually suck at something else. That's just how the brain works. Think about the bad handwriting of doctors and engineers—they're *famous* for marginal manual dexterity, but have huge brains for spatial reasoning and long-term memory.

If I spent all day trying to excel at design, I'd be wasting my brainpower. It makes a million times more sense for me to focus on channeling my superpower toward getting potential clients, partners, and investors excited about our business.

Do what you're best at. It's what you love. And better yet, it creates what people call a virtuous cycle. Love it more, do it more—get even better!

You'll free up more time to be a better human being. You'll have more fun. You'll create excellence. Superpowers are what set the superheroes apart from everyone else. What's yours?

BE A FOLLOWER

IN BOTH BUSINESS AND IN LIFE, YOU USUALLY have to be a follower before you can become a leader.

I learned this when I was young, skipping grades and hanging out with my older brother and his friends. Given that I was generally several years younger than the kids I hung around with, guess who was not always the top dog?

It wasn't always easy for me to stay confident in those situations, but it was so much fun hanging with kids who could do things I couldn't that I lost interest in trying to be the leader of the pack. I accepted myself for the follower I was, and let myself get comfortable with the role I was in.

When you are comfortable with your place in the food chain, people tend to like you. It's hard not to like people who like themselves (in a non-smug way). It's hard not to like people who aren't trying to prove anything or one-up anybody; it's easy to be around them. Don't you often like to be around younger, less accomplished people even more than you do some of your peers, because you don't see them as competition? They appear more benign and less threatening. And because they don't take themselves too seriously, they can be so much cooler and relaxed than a lot of people.

That never changes, no matter what level you rise to. Even so, there's always at least a little fear factor in being the underdog. People with power and status can intimidate you.

I learned, though, that even if people are at a lofty level, they are still just people, like you and me.

When I started Kiip, I had to pitch lots of big honchos at big brands, and it's hard to walk into those meetings without a few butterflies in your stomach, especially if you're barely older than some of their kids. Back then, our start-up—like every start-up in the beginning—wasn't much of anything, and that made me the (very young) CEO of Not Much of Anything, Inc. It turned out that wasn't such a bad thing.

Sure, some established companies had a big head start on us, and they were always going to be bigger and more experienced. So we said, "Okay, that's cool—we'll be David and they can be Goliath." And we all know how that story ends.

Because here's the thing: Since we were smaller, Kiip could be nimble and quick, and do things bigger players in the ad space couldn't, like building things that didn't look like the typical ad. Or using entirely different metrics. Or flying in the face of conventional advertising thinking. We could also make our clients feel like they were almost a part of our team—that the level of service we could give them could make us almost an extension of them. We could also show that being early customers of ours was an advantage and a strength for them, because it proved to the world how innovative they were. On the timeline, we were followers, but when it came to innovation, we became leaders.

The power of being a follower also works in the personal realm. I don't have to try to walk into a meeting on the eightieth floor of a Manhattan megalith and pretend to be equal to the CEOs twice my age. Instead I've learned how to make my youth work for me, as I'll talk more about in Cheat 20. I realized that being young is great if you look at the positives instead of the negatives. It gives me a fresh perspective that older execs value. They expect me to be innovative and to think outside of the box. Youth is especially valuable in advertising, where practically every brand is obsessed with reaching millennials. Their take was, who better to learn from than a millennial himself?

Sure, some big-time business titans like to intimidate people, and they're good at it. But most of them don't even try. They don't have to. The majority that I've met are the coolest people ever, and you immediately feel comfortable around them. That down-to-earth personality is a big part of why they're there. It's a mark of a great leader.

So when I go into a meeting with any person of power now, I go in with the perspective that I'm just meeting with a normal person, like somebody I'd meet on the subway, and I try to have a normal conversation with him or her. I don't set myself up for failure by being afraid.

After all, all the most powerful leaders out there started out as followers—and look where they are now.

DON'T TRY TO WIN A HUMILITY CONTEST

NOT THAT THERE IS SUCH A THING AS A HUMILity contest—by definition, humble people wouldn't enter, would they?

When somebody once asked Warren Buffett to give a speech on humility—since he's the de facto winner of the humility contest among billionaires—he said, "Isn't giving a speech about humility an oxymoron?"

Too many people work too hard at being humble, and it shows. They're so demonstrably self-effacing and flattering of others that it just doesn't ring true. Call it the vanity of humility, the ultimate oxymoron. You know the type I'm talking about here. There's just something off about them.

Warren Buffett recently offered a good definition of humility at an event devoted to advice for CEOs under age thirty. He said humility is "knowing the edges of your own competency," and added that he'd rather be somebody with an IQ of 130 who thinks it's 125 than somebody with an IQ of 180 who thinks it's 200.

My goal in this area is simply to be the kind of person that people like to hang out with. Humility isn't something you can engineer; it's just a matter of being true to who you are as you grow. That's why introspection is so key. You need to keep asking yourself: "Who am I really? Why am I doing the things I do? What makes me feel comfortable in my own skin?"

Ben Franklin, who polished his introspection to the degree of genius, had a simple habit for self-improvement that inadvertently helped him stay humble: He made a list at the end of the day about things he could have done better. The point of it wasn't to become more humble, but just to do the things on the list better. That's why it helped keep a lid on his ego. It reminded him that there are always things he could do better.

If you can stay introspective, you naturally end up being yourself—and the real you is always very humble.

There's a saying, "Be yourself, because everyone else is taken," and it's so true. You are yourself, whether you want to be or not.

When you are yourself, you don't need to work on being humble, any more than Franklin did. When you achieve the greater goal of being comfortable with yourself, you won't need to worry about trying to be humble after you achieve some great thing, like all the movie stars who win an award and say, "I've never felt more humble." Humility is not something you actually want to brag about. Real humility comes while you're still working on your achievement—it's not an after-the-fact thing. You don't wake up in the morning and go, "Oh, I'm going to be humble now." Of course movie stars get humble after a while—they're fucking rich and famous, so they can afford to be. Or at least afford to act like they are.

So let's end this with some Shakespeare: "This above all: to thine own self be true, / And it must follow, as the night the day, / Thou canst not then be false to any man."

DON'T OUTSMART YOURSELF!

M Y MOM WAS ALWAYS THERE FOR ME WHEN I was a kid, cheering me on at things like my hockey games, giving me advice, and keeping a close eye on how I was interacting with other kids, just to make sure I got started on the right path. A great parent—and a great leader too—is someone who is so in tune with how you're developing that it's easy for them to help you make course corrections on the fly. One of the biggest corrections she ever pointed out to me was: "You can't outsmart everyone. If you try to, you'll only outsmart yourself."

As usual, she was right. She knew I was intelligent—thanks to some good genes from her and my dad, and some hard work of my own—and she realized that smart people tend to overthink things. When we do, we tell ourselves it's a product of intellect, but it's really a product of fear, and it's one of the worst traits you can bring to your work.

When you do, you usually end up thinking in circles, like the smart character Vizzini in *The Princess Bride*, who thinks his enemy is trying to poison him with some wine that he puts at each of their table settings. He knows a clever man wouldn't drink the wine in front of him and would demand to switch glasses, but he also knows his enemy knows that, and so he should therefore not switch glasses. But then he thinks, "Wait, this enemy also knows *that*" . . . etc., etc. So he goes around in circles until he arrives at his brilliant conclusion, drinks his wine, and dies.

The streets of Silicon Valley are littered with people who thought of so many contingency plans and potential scenarios that nothing got done. Part of the problem is that most smart people who are part of this industry got tossed into the mental pressure cooker of academia, where overthinking becomes an art form. But really, since when does success in academia translate into success in the real world?

So instead of overthinking, why not try overdoing?

I could go into a long discourse on the exact significance of that advice. But why overthink it?

MAKE AGE YOUR FRIEND!

SOMETIMES I START SPEECHES TO AUDIENCES of very accomplished people who look like they're older than me—which is easy, since I'm twenty-five and look even younger—with something like, "You're probably wondering why you're here listening to a twelve-year-old Asian kid."

That self-deprecating line does two things. It says (1) "You guys are cool, and sometimes I wish I was a little older, like you." And (2) "I'm cool too, and sometimes you probably wish you were a little younger, like me."

But don't worry: You don't have to be twenty-five to use this cheat. If you know how to use your age to your advantage, there's no bad age to be.

That truth gets lost in the tech culture, because there's a perceived chasm between young people, who grew up in the e-world, and older people, who didn't.

Of course, this isn't just a function of our high-tech world; there's always been a perceived gulf between old and young, and every generation comes up with a new rendition of it. In the sixties, when the boomers were the kids, it was the culture chasm between the flower children and their World War II–era parents; after that it was the gap between the aging boomers and Gen X, and today it's the middle-aged Gen Xers versus, well, guys like me.

John Hayes, the chief marketing officer of American Express (an investor in Kiip), is somebody who bridges the generation gap gracefully and shows other people how. When I met him I thought he was in his late forties, but I just Googled him and learned that he's sixty, and spent the last year learning how to code for iPhone apps. He gained a lot of respect from his team for being an older guy who can code; in his case, his age works in his favor.

He's a guy who knows not only that old dogs can learn new tricks but also that new tricks aren't the real key to staying current. Recently he said, "Too often we tend to think of change in a very singular mind-set: as technology. But technology is not the root cause—it's an effect. The real driver of societal change is society itself, not your smartphone."

Progress, in other words, has no age—or at least not one that's particularly relevant. So whatever part of life you're in, there's always a way to spin your age to your advantage.

You learn how little age matters in a microsecond when you touch down at the airport in San Francisco, the world's petri dish for start-ups. When I go back home to SF after a trip to the real world, still carrying the feeling of being the youngest guy on the planet, it isn't long before I walk down the street and see somebody I know and think: "Man, here's a kid who's five years younger than me that just raised more money than me, and is building ideas that are probably even cooler than mine. And, damn, he's probably getting more girls too. I'm too old for this shit!"

Which gets me where? Nowhere. It's all a matter of perspective, so why worry about it?

To my investors, the least interesting thing about me is my age. The same days they talk to me, they probably talk to CEOs younger than me—who also have PhDs.

That doesn't stop me from spinning my age as a hook to the media, though. As I mention in Cheat 33, when the press mentions me, they usually tag my age. But there's a pretty obvious shelf life to that hook. They generally tie it to the questionable concept that only young people can understand a young market, but so what? When I'm too old for the youth angle, I'll start to play the experience card.

A friend of mine who's officially an old guy but doesn't act like it says that he spent the first half of his career lying about how old he was and the second half lying about how young he was. That's a cheat within a cheat: Don't act your age. If you act stodgy when you're old, or silly when you're young, you're playing into the hands of negative stereotyping, and aging yourself out of business.

The other great thing about age is that it tends to naturally put you in different life phases, each of which has advantages. Like a lot of people in their early twenties, I don't have a family to take care of, so I can stay out all night, grab a 6:00 a.m. flight, and come home whenever. Nobody to tuck in. No garage door left open to worry about.

Nobody says to me, "You're a fucking asshole for being intentionally irresponsible, and always putting yourself first." They say, "Live it up! Enjoy that freedom while you've got it." I'll take that advice any day.

But I've got buddies who are a little older, and being a dad and a husband is one of their greatest motivators—because you'll always work a little harder for somebody you love than you will for yourself. Their families are also their emotional anchors and the people they trust most. Some of them even use their kids and nieces and nephews as their primary panel for market research. These guys don't have to think about dating, or try to impress people, or worry about being lonely. There's freedom in that too.

So embrace your age, without acting out the stereotypes. You'll only have the age you are now once, so you might as well take advantage of it.

TUNE OUT!

I WAS ONCE RIDING A TOUR BUS IN THE SERENE Halong Bay area, in northern Vietnam, where scattered rock monoliths rise out of the bay like granite skyscrapers, feeling the wind in my face, listening to the calls of magnificent birds—and trying to ignore the tour guide's cell phone ringing. Again. And again.

Finally he turned the phone off and looked at me. "I do not like it," he sighed. "My girlfriend keeps calling, and I don't have time to respond."

"Which she doesn't like, right?"

"Right."

I felt his newfound pain. Part of the new e-etiquette is that if you don't respond to somebody—whether it's your significant other, your business partner, or a client or customer—in a matter of hours (or minutes, or seconds), you're blowing them off. So you're either a slave to your devices or the bad guy. What a shitty choice.

Like it or not, though, it's a by-product of the information-rich world we live in today. According to Eric Schmidt, who used to be the CEO of Google, between the beginning of civilization and 2003, humankind created five exabytes, or five quintillion bytes, of information. Now we create that much every two days.

Or put another way, in just the last two years, 90 percent of all the data that's ever existed has been generated. More scary stats: Americans absorb twelve hours of information every day outside the office. Office workers spend 28 percent of their time answering email. People send or receive an average of thirty-five texts every day.

This information overload is causing short-term memory loss, higher stress, and worse health, and it costs the economy a fortune. It's become such an epidemic that we now even have clever terms for too much shit penetrating your brain—like "infobesity" or "infoxication"—but in plain English it's called a pain in the ass, and a huge handicap. And it's not even good for productivity or for our relationships; after all, when we're so busy responding to texts and emails, when can we find the time to be creative? It turns us into Pavlovian dogs. You know the feeling: The second an email comes in, your blood pressure rises a bit and you think, "Fuck, somebody wants something." And that makes you both stressed out and resentful.

So here's a cheat worth remembering, if you still have any room in your memory: Tune out!

Stop telling yourself that intelligence is based on knowing what's happening at this very minute. Stop trying to be in touch with everybody all the time. Don't feel like you've got to notify the world every time you have lunch. All that stuff is like a drug. But like any drug, it can be hard to go cold turkey, and realistically most of us would have a hard time maintaining both our careers and our relationships if we went totally off the grid. The key is to use the information drug only in moderation.

I'm working on it myself. Even though I fly all the time, I don't do any communication on flights. On my day off, I don't take work calls. I permanently turned off email notifications on my phone. I batch my emails and address them only when I actually have the time, so I can at least set the tempo instead of being a slave to other people's agendas.

People don't think about this, but every time they send you a text or email, they're taking away your time without your permission. It's a little like they're barging into your office without an appointment.

We're obviously in a new era of mobile communication—which, ironically, is my primary area of business. But that makes me even more attuned to the fact that we need to control it before it controls us. I am in the mobile advertising field, but my mission is to offer people promotions and information about products that people *want*, and choose, instead of just sticking it in their face.

We're all pressured to stay wired, but bending over and taking whatever information people throw at us is not the way to deal with it. Stand up for your right to some peace, quiet, alone time, family time, fun time, and creative time.

Ask people to give you some space. The people you really want to have in your life will be fine with that. The people you don't want in your life will get the message, and to them I say good riddance.

When you show respect for yourself and your time, other people will start showing respect for it as well.

MAKE YOUR OWN FUN

A S WE LEARNED IN A *MARY POPPINS* SONG, IN
ev'ry job that must be done / there is an element of fun /
You find the fun and SNAP! / The job's a game. Or something
like that.

That's one more reason to be your own boss in the golden age
of entrepreneurship: You get to make your own fun.

Sure, some people are lucky enough to have a boss who knows
that work and fun can coexist. If you're not, you need to find a
new boss, and maybe that boss is you.

Some people think fun is incompatible with a work ethic. But
this couldn't be further from the truth. After all, it's called a work
ethic, not a suffering ethic.

The ability to have fun is one of those classic cheats that I
talk about all the time. Remember the old saying "Fun is fundamental"? Well, it's true. Why do you think the writers of the
Declaration of Independence ranked the pursuit of happiness
right up there with life and liberty? Because they knew that the
deep-seated, primal need to enjoy what you do, without some
tyrant—petty or otherwise—stomping on your soul, is a fundamental human right.

I have fun at my job, and I make sure that the people I work with are having fun too. If they're not, they'll lose their interest and energy. It goes without saying that not every aspect of a job is fun; but if you've even *thought* the phrase "My job is no fun," then you need a new job. If you're doing it right, having a job shouldn't feel like having just "a job." Life is too short, and careers are even shorter.

The single best way to have fun with your job is to take it upon yourself, regardless of your job description, to find something new in it every day. Kiip learning, kiip trying different tactics, kiip growing, and kiip moving.

When you do things too mechanically or repetitively, you take the fun out of them. Every time I do a presentation or even have a meeting, I always explore ways to do something that's different, just to give people the feeling of: I wasn't expecting that! Not only does it make things more interesting for me, they like that feeling, and they appreciate me for offering them something new.

We are all, at heart, explorers. Old gets old. New is fun.

We're also survivors, and we know that if we come to somebody with the same old thing so often that they know what's coming, we'll be instantly boring and eminently disposable.

If you're having fun at your job, you won't pay much attention to things like long hours or even low earnings. You'll do amazing work. Your fun will be contagious, and your workday will be the main event, instead of another boring opening act to suffer through before the weekend.

Here's a one-step mini-cheat to having fun: Let go and be yourself. If you do, you won't be looking over your shoulder for trouble, the way people are when they're putting on an act, so you probably won't find any. You'll be loose, funny, open, and free.

Ideas will come naturally. Friends will flock to you. Your superiors will see you as an equal.

Part of being yourself, though, is being in a job that welcomes that attitude. Not every boss is enlightened—as I'm sure you've noticed.

Don't let yourself get shoved into a job where you can't be yourself, just because of money or status.

When you're working at the job you should be working at, it feels right. It feels natural. Your days will have a buzz to them.

I can't tell you what that job is. It might even be hard for you to predict what it is.

When you're in it, though, you'll know it.

That will be the job that will take you to your peak moments of opportunity. And that will be fun.

DON'T TRY TO BE BETTER THAN EVERYBODY ELSE

I HAVE SOME GOOD NEWS FOR YOU. IF YOU WANT to win in this world, you don't have to be better than everybody. You just have to be better than your immediate competitor.

Funny parable: Two guys are in the woods. Out of nowhere comes a grizzly bear! He's mean! He's hungry! He lumbers toward them. One guy sits down to put on his sneakers. Other guy says, "Shit, dude, you can't outrun that bear." First guy replies, "I don't have to outrun the bear. I just have to outrun you."

It works the same in business. If you happen to be hanging out with high achievers and meet somebody who's inordinately successful but not remotely the brightest, most driven person in the room, it tells you one thing: He's at least a little smarter and more tenacious than his closest competitors.

That's all it takes.

A lot of people get caught up in the hero worship of super-amazing people—Musk, Page, Bezos, Jobs—and try to compare themselves with them. Don't. It's irrelevant.

It's a waste of time to compare yourself to the upper echelon of the whole world. The world is too big and you're too small. You'll always lose, and when you do, you'll feel like a loser.

If you work at a major corporation, don't even compare yourself to the CEO or COO, because it's generally an exercise in futility. Compare yourself to the person in the office or the cubicle next to yours, or to the person a level or two above you. *That's* your real competition.

That said, oftentimes, even your closest competitors are irrelevant. Because ultimately, you're only competing against one person: yourself.

It's like my parents told me a long time ago: You're competing with yourself more than you're competing with anyone else. So as long as you're a better version of yourself every day, you're fine.

For creative people—like me, and probably like you—there's more than enough success to go around. Creative people don't play a zero-sum game. We try to help other people get what we have, and if we need more, we create more: as a team, with the people we've helped. If you can be a better you every day, you can win the race.

DO IT YOUR WAY

HERE'S AN EXAMPLE OF SERENDIPITY—AKA luck with your eyes open: I was walking down the street with a few guys and we bumped into some mutual friends. One of my buddies said, "Adam, this is Brian Wong—he just got laid off at Digg, and he's starting his own company."

Adam D'Augelli stuck out his hand and said, "What are you starting?"

Adam was then an associate at the five-year-old venture capital firm True Ventures, which focused on finding tech start-ups in their earliest stages.

"Well, I can't really say," I said, "because we're still forming it, but let's meet up sometime."

Adam is one of those people who you can tell are smart just from the clarity and focus they project, and he seemed like a good guy, friendly and fit. I knew I'd at least get some good advice from him.

A week later we had coffee and I told him about my idea for a mobile advertising company that rewards consumers with free products during moments of achievements in gaming. My reasoning was that almost everybody hates ads, but they love achievement and reward, so it would create a consumer-product bond.

Shortly after that he brought me to his partners, from whom I hoped to find out even more about how to get investors, and they're like: "How much are you raising?" I had no idea. But I said, "I don't know—$300,000 or $400,000."

A week later I came back and they gave me a term sheet for $300,000. I was so blown away that I said about the dumbest thing I could—which was also probably the smartest, because it was honest: "This is ridiculous. You're actually giving me $300,000, and I don't even have a company yet?"

So that's the easy way to find investors. Just walk down the street.

It helps, though, to walk down the street with an insanely good idea, experience in a business similar to the one you want to start, a friend whose friend is an investor, a ton of ambition, honesty—and pure (*Cheat Code*–worthy) luck, augmented by the ability to keep your eyes open and know a good opportunity when you see it.

I thought about it, and told True Ventures that I wanted to make room for some individual investors, or angel investors: wealthy people who would put in their own money. It was a tricky proposition, because making room for more angel investors meant that the True Ventures ownership position would be reduced.

I was lucky, and they said okay. They put in $200,000, and we began to seek another $100,000 from some angel investors.

Adam and his partners realized that was good for everyone. Adam's investment, of course, fed confidence to the venerable boys' club of investors in the Valley, including the angels.

I skipped a common source of initial investment: seed money from friends and family. That wasn't something I felt good about, because I knew I'd have too much remorse if things didn't work out. A friends-and-family phase of investment is a more practical approach if your friends or family are wealthy. It's also reasonable if they completely understand the risks and absolutely insist on getting in on the ground floor, as refusing someone's rational desire to share risk and reward can cause hard feelings.

When I started approaching angels, we already had a few customers, and we were expecting more. We established some early goals for ourselves, and—as planned—we reached them. That impressed the angels, even though we'd set the goals ourselves. So that's a mini-cheat: Set realistic goals, meet and beat them, and let the world know you did.

Our key angels, along with entrepreneur-turned-investor Paige Craig, included Rohan Oza, the former CMO of Vitaminwater; Keith Belling, the founder of Popchips; Joe Stump, the lead architect of Digg, who made sure it would scale properly; and Ryan Swagar, a cofounder of Venture51. They were all supersmart, young guys who saw the potential in a company that could change advertising into something people like.

Our second set of investors—still in the A round—came after we were rolling, but still quite early in Kiip's evolution. One of the most important meetings happened at a gathering of my fellow Canadians who'd moved to California. Believe it or not, there are about 350,000 Canadians in California, making us about 1 percent of the population. The event, C100, was for Canadian entrepreneurs, and there I met Lars Leckie, of the venture capital firm Hummer Winblad. They invested $4 million.

Lars is equally adept at business and technology, holds several patents, started as a computer game hacker, and founded Novariant, a company that focuses on GPS and robotics.

By the time I was nineteen, we'd raised almost $5 million—a

record for a teenager. That record, in and of itself, represented about a million dollars' worth of credibility and publicity.

You're smart enough to see *Cheat Code* themes emerging from this narrative without me spelling them out. The big ones are:

- Find people you don't want to just make money with but be closely linked with for a long time.
- Get your ass out into the world, where you'll know people and be known.
- Be yourself to such a degree that it's hard *not* to trust you.
- Always stay more full of fun than of fear.
- Look for great ideas and grab them by the throat when they appear.
- Don't let a job layoff or any other problem undermine you.
- Know serendipity when you see it.
- And, of course, walk down the street.

The overarching *Cheat Code* mega-theme: There is no one way. There are lots of ways.

I did it my way. You do it yours.

TAKE A SPLURGE DAY

I F WE LEARNED ANYTHING FROM THE CLASSIC Stanley Kubrick film *The Shining*, it was "All work and no play makes Johnny a maniacal ax murderer."

As those who have seen the film will recall, Jack Nicholson's workaholic mind-set was ultimately of no value to him—nor to his family.

That's why I believe in regularly having a splurge day.

The most successful people know that taking time to recharge is the only way to stay on your A-game for an extended period of time. I don't have the time or desire at this stage of my career to take extended vacations, so I pick at least one day every month for a mini-vacation of cramming in as many of my favorite things as possible.

It's a cheat that's kept me almost completely free from homicidal tendencies. I strongly recommend it to people with high-intensity careers, and even to anyone with a moderately stressful job.

So what do I do on my splurge day? I unplug all my devices, hang out at my favorite spot in the park, go eat brunch at my fa-

vorite restaurant, and eat ice cream at my favorite place. I just do
everything as my *favorite* everything, and it's awesome.

If you don't have these splurge days, or your own version of them, you will inevitably burn out.

Best of all, even an occasional splurge day gives you something to look forward to every day as you're working long hours at the office or getting all too acquainted with the business travel lounge at your local airport. As Jane Austen said, the anticipation of happiness is happiness itself.

Every once in a while, instead of sitting in the park and eating ice cream, I use my splurge day to simply catch up on sleep. This is equally important. As you read in Cheat 3, even Energizer bunnies like me can't *go go go go* forever without occasionally recharging the battery.

My most recent splurge day was when I came back from one of my body-hammering trips—you know, the kind where the time zones all merged into Brian Daylight Time. As soon as I hit home, I slept thirty hours. I wish I could remember it. It must have been great. Doesn't matter. My body remembers. That's good enough.

The body will tell you when it needs a break. Listen to it!

BE LEGENDARY

FOR YOU TO ACHIEVE PHENOMENAL, ENDURING success, you should inspire so much faith in the people you work with that you become a legend among them.

It may be easier than you think.

You don't need to be legendary at everything—that's impossible, and not even productive, because it creates the onus of being a one-man team.

Instead, pick one of your superpowers, and be the person who is always done ahead of schedule, or always cool under pressure, or always coming up with novel solutions, or always the most tenacious, or always nicest to everybody.

It doesn't matter what your superpower is, as long as you're so amazing at it that it's the stuff of legends.

The same attribute should apply to your company. Think about how the most successful companies are legendary for being one of the most (take your pick): innovative (Apple, as one example), trusted (Disney), stable (Berkshire Hathaway), futuristic (Google), or patient (Amazon).

Let's consider for the moment Amazon, for its legendary patience:

Amazon is so damn patient—placing so little emphasis on current profitability—that some people call it the "Dangerous Dynasty." In an era when CEOs live and die on their quarterly reports, Amazon's Jeff Bezos is legendary for practically ignoring them.

Amazon isn't even very interested in the profit margins that it reaps on individual products. That's because Bezos created a culture that focuses on one thing: long-range domination of global, retail e-commerce.

Year after year, profits are regarded as almost an afterthought. This is why, even though Amazon ran in the red for its first seven years and endured a losing year as recently as 2012, its stock is now running in the range of $500 per share—because people are absolutely convinced that Bezos, with his eye on the horizon, sees things that the rest of us don't. Investors are sure that Bezos's long-term vision will solve pesky little problems, like not making a profit.

That's the stuff of legends.

Bezos's fabled modus operandi almost borders, for some, on religious faith—or at least fervor. People view it as a way to explain life and establish values.

Legend spawns legend, and one of the great urban legends of Jeff Bezos is that he's building a Millennium Clock in the desert that will last for ten thousand years. Bezos believes that the quixotic, chaotic pace of technology has created a false sense of time, compressing it with a power akin to that of a black hole, where the increasing acceleration eventually makes everything literally happen at once. Therefore, Bezos says, "It's going to be increasingly important, over time, for humanity to take a longer-term view of its future."

The legend about him building the Millennium Clock is true. Sort of. In actuality, the clock is being built by a nonprofit called the Long Now Foundation, which has about 3,300 members. It's being built five hundred feet down in a Texas mountain, under the direction of a supercomputer developer (and Milton Bradley toymaker) named Danny Hillis, the cofounder of Thinking Machines, Inc., who created the foundation and conceived of the clock. Bezos just chipped in—to the tune of $40 million, though, making him the biggest donor.

But it doesn't matter if that's his real message or if he's not really the driving force behind the clock's creation. What matters is that Jeff Bezos has become a legend and carried his company with him. Whatever he does at this point will make him even more legendary on many levels.

Bezos is larger than life as we know it. His company, by extension, is larger than business as we know it. Bezos plus Amazon is more like a movement, a moral code, or, to some, a religion. No matter what happens to Amazon over the next hundred years, the legend of Jeff Bezos and his company will live long, and large.

You too can be legendary, no matter what industry you're in or what kind of work you do. But as they say, Rome wasn't built in a day.

Sometimes it pays to dream in smaller chunks—as long as you dream every day. Devour the world in bite-size pieces. They'll get bigger all the time.

Celebrate every new rung on the ladder! If you do—no matter how slow your climb—you'll have the confidence to keep going. That's a golden asset. You'll exude the aura of somebody who's on the way up, and when you start inspiring that perception, it happens.

Life is long, and the race, as they say, doesn't always go to the swift.

If you want to become the stuff of legends, the key is to do everything just a little bit better than everybody else. That's how you cheat your way to incredible success, one day at a time.

BE
UNFORGETTABLE

LEARN TIPS AND TRICKS
AROUND PR, BUILD
YOUR BRAND, AND GET
ATTENTION FOR YOURSELF
AND YOUR IDEAS.

MAKE THINGS LOOK CONSISTENTLY PRETTY: THE POWER OF APPEARANCE 1.0

NO MATTER WHAT BUSINESS YOU'RE IN OR what you're selling, your promise is your brand, and your brand is your promise. You're telling people what you will do for them, and your success in large part hinges upon how appealing that promise is. Kiip's promise is "We create advertising that people actually like." That's a huge promise, and it's a primary reason that our company has been as successful as it is.

Your brand, though, is only as good as its presentation: how it looks, sounds, and feels. Its presentation is the beginning of your promise. Some people might think that presentation takes a backseat to substance. But like it or not, presentation matters, and if you offer the world a brand that is not sensually attractive, you're going to have a hard time getting people to pay attention to the substance of what you have to offer.

Evolutionary psychologists say that humans are programmed to differentiate a threat from a non-threat in two seconds. And today, with attention spans shorter than ever, that's about as long as you have to make a good visual first impression.

I started my career in design. I was the kid who got his hands on a copy of Photoshop at the age of eleven and learned from tutorials online. You should have seen some of the cool stuff I handed in during high school, and I'm convinced my strong presentation skills were a big part of what enabled me to leapfrog grades, which landed me in college at age fourteen. Sure, the content of my reports probably had something to do with it, but to be honest, the content wasn't always as fabulous as the way it was presented. Everything I turned in always looked fantastic because of the design skills I taught myself from tutorials on the Internet.

My projects didn't need to be the best in the world; they just needed to look better than the next guy's (another cheat). I handed in the same report on dinosaurs as everybody else, but mine had an extra-sexy cover page that looked slick and professional. That was the Brian Brand: The Early Years.

The Brian Brand projects looked so good that they *promised to be good*, and that became a self-fulfilling prophecy, setting the stage for further achievement.

I was the kid who always added graphics and perfected the look of all of my class presentations, and it served me so well that I've carried it with me throughout my career as an entrepreneur. Of course, I'm in advertising, which is a lot about presentation— but I would argue that presentation is equally important for virtually any other type of business.

The fact is, we're visual, sense-driven creatures, and we're not the only species that is. It's telling that the phrase "the birds and the bees"—referring to two types of creatures that are both fundamentally animated by beauty, whether flowers, fragrances, or the splendor of colored feathers—has become a euphemism for love and reproduction: the essence of life.

In regard to people, I'll be the first to admit that you really can't, as the cliché goes, judge a book by its cover; it's what's on the inside that counts. But that truth simply doesn't apply to things like presentations, reports, websites, logos, and even little details like how you space paragraphs in your emails.

When it comes to visual things, we're all shallow. We make snap judgments. We like beauty—in flowers, in art, in architecture, in bodies, in faces. This tendency is, after all, a part of nature.

Beauty catches our attention. It seeps into our memory, into our subconscious. So if it's brand recognition you're after, good visual presentation isn't just something that's nice to have. It's a must. Who can forget the beauty of a peacock, or even the NBC peacock logo? That's the brand that helped make NBC an early leader in color TV. The visual signal was so significant at the time—although people don't remember that, because nobody owns a black-and-white TV anymore!

This cheat works almost every time, for almost every kind of brand. If shit looks sleek and sexy, people will be primed to see and judge it in a better light. That's a time-and-time-again truism. The slicker a brand is, the more you trust it—and the better you remember it.

Visuals matter even in something as simple as an email. If an email is horridly formatted, with big-ass paragraphs, no spacing, and a tiny generic font—or, worse, huge letters and garish, in-your-face colors—you just don't want to read it, and when you do, you're already expecting not to like it. You think (maybe consciously, maybe not): "They didn't care enough to make it look good, so I'm supposed to waste my precious time on it?"

You can only imagine the response Kiip would get from our pitches if we designed *anything* that was not aesthetically pleasing. Actually, you probably couldn't imagine it, because there would be no Kiip. That's part of why our design director, Amadeus Demarzi, is my cofounder. Design is absolutely crucial to the success of our brand, and to yours as well, no matter what that brand is. When you look consistently good, it helps get you in the habit of *being* consistently good. People come to expect that from you—and so you come to expect it from yourself.

So here's the cheat in a nutshell:

To be memorable, look good, look different. That's your brand.

When you look consistently good, it helps get you in the habit of *being* consistently good. People come to expect that from you—and so do you.

KIIP CHANGING YOUR LOOK: THE POWER OF APPEARANCE 2.0

ONE THEME THAT RUNS THROUGH MANY OF the cheats in this book is to be careful never to get complacent. Even once you've made all your company's visuals, from your logo to your website to your emails, look consistently pretty, you've got to match the march of time with tweaks that keep your look fresh.

So once you've nailed your presentation, the next step is to tweak it. Don't get in a rut. Get people to expect the unexpected, and they'll be more interested in seeing you again. It builds your "you brand."

The same thing goes for whatever your product is. Let's start with emails. I once hired a sales guy who would end all of his emails with a random animated GIF appended to the bottom of his post—something like a dancing chicken or some funny cat video, but always something different and memorable. You always opened this guy's emails just to see what he'd appended.

No matter what business you're in, it's super-important to tweak your company's various appearances on a regular basis and to be absolutely certain that your look reflects the forward momentum of your brand.

If you don't keep adjusting your company's visuals, people will think you're stuck in a rut, even if there's evidence that you're not. On a subconscious level, looks don't lie.

Similarly, how your company describes itself *visually* can be as eloquent as the *words* you choose to describe it.

If your looks don't portray progress, it actually undermines your progress, especially in businesses that convey their promise with visuals-driven media, as so many do these days.

As time goes on and your technology and techniques evolve by leaps and bounds, you want your visuals to reflect it—your decks, your website, your logo, everything.

In short, you need to constantly update your look in order to signal to your customers and clients that you're keeping up with their demand for improvement and innovation—that you're evolving to meet new needs as they arise.

Kiip's initial product look was very basic—just an email field and an image—but as we added new functions over time, we aggressively reflected those improvements visually. We also made our design more appealing for the larger screens that were beginning to dominate the market, and we tweaked our interface to make it look more like Apple's design, so it would fit in better on Apple devices. Another thing that told people that Kiip was on the move was our addition of background images for rewards, which made them feel more integrated with the app. We then showed the industry what rewards could look like on the future generation of connected devices—to help our clients imagine the future with us.

Even as I write this, we're in the midst of a complete overhaul of the design. And it won't be the last.

Facebook is famous for design changes (or infamous, among the customers who love to hate Facebook's changes). There were so many times when Facebook changed and people went: "Fuck, why did they move the button? Why did they do all this shit just when I'm getting familiar with it?" But despite these complaints, Facebook's continuous design evolution is a big reason the network has continued to thrive as the uncontested market leader while so many of its competitors have fizzled and died.

Facebook changes their look to get their users used to the fact that there will always be changes to its functions to meet the demands of the times. Change is absolutely essential, especially in technology. True, some of Facebook's changes may be of more benefit to the company than to its users, but that doesn't matter. Facebook is training people to expect change as an organic process of technology as well as of life. However, Facebook tweaks in a controlled way—not too many, not too fast, but always something. That way, they have the ability to introduce and test new options without igniting a big revolt.

The company I used to work for, the news aggregator Digg, didn't handle design change nearly as well, and it almost buried them.

For a long time, as Digg's success built upon itself, the company took the attitude of "Our user base is so loyal that we might lose people if we change." Then, with little warning, in the summer of 2010 they pushed out their V4 release, which fundamentally changed the entire look of the site overnight, and it exploded in their faces. They killed their policy of embedding ads that looked very similar to the stories, and started teaming with media outlets and celebrities to create publisher accounts. The too-big-too-fast changes also created a bunch of technical glitches, which of course nobody liked. Their whole community of partners and users got pissed beyond belief. And because Digg's bet was so big, they couldn't gracefully back away. Within a few months, they were losing so much money, they had to lay off more than one-third of their staff. It was a bloodbath. Good people lost their jobs. Profits evaporated.

The point is it was smart for Digg to make some changes to the look and feel of their site, but they shouldn't have totally overhauled their entire business and design structure all at once. And they sure as hell shouldn't have bet the farm on it.

Progress, in other words, is crucial. But it needs to be nuanced and controlled, and its visual presentation should reflect as much.

Don't make the mistake, though, of thinking that you can fake the existence of progress with nothing but a new look. There are companies in our mobile advertising space that are still, to be blunt about it, shoveling the same shit, but they have rebranded themselves to try to trick people into thinking that they have a new product when they really don't. Customers will see right through this. Great visuals or no great visuals, you still need to continue to make the product better, not just the look.

When you achieve real progress, you don't have to trick people.

But you do have to show them—with irresistible visuals—that progress has been made.

DRESS THE PART: THE POWER OF APPEARANCE 3.0

KEEPING THE LOOK OF YOUR COMPANY BRAND fresh and powerful is critically important, but never forget that you've got two brands. One is your company, and the other is the brand known as you.

How you look counts. It always has. It always will. If that sounds shallow, I apologize—but these cheats can't help you succeed if they're not brutally honest.

The good news is that you can project a strong personal brand by following the same rules I just outlined for your professional brand: look good, look different, and keep updating your look, but gradually; no big makeovers overnight. You've probably gone back to your hometown at one time or another and run into some guy who looked like he was wearing the same sweatshirt he wore in high school. Not too impressive, is it? You're afraid to ask him what he's been up to lately, because he'll probably say something like, "Same old thing . . . you know." He looks exactly the same as he did when he was seventeen and bagging groceries at the local grocery store, and so you assume his career never advanced much further. You'd probably be right.

What if you actually have been moving ahead in life, though, but still show up in the same old sweatshirt—to work, a party, or a high school reunion? If you present yourself the same way you did years ago, you're telling people you haven't changed, even if you have.

But it's not enough to just look *good*. If you want to stand out, you also need to look *different*. But don't be different just to be different. Do it to be you.

Part of my personal brand now is that I don't wear the same outfits that everyone else wears—not for the sake of making a statement, but just because I wear whatever I want to wear (which I suppose is a statement in itself, but an authentic one). If I'm going to a big meeting where everyone's going to be in a suit and tie, I'll come in wearing a blazer or polo or whatever—cool shoes, cool socks. You should have seen the socks I wore on the cover of the Young Millionaires edition of *Entrepreneur* magazine.

When you present yourself authentically, people go: "Dude, I have a lot of respect for that, because you're so comfortable!" People admire you when you're you. They don't trust you if you're trying to look like somebody else—and if you're trying to look like everybody else, good luck.

When I started taking business classes, about ten years ago, they trained us to wear our sharpest suits when we went into an interview or any other kind of important meeting, partly to make people take you seriously, and partly so you'd take yourself seriously. The thinking was, if you had a killer suit on, you'd psych yourself into believing you were a mature, hard-nosed business person. It was good advice . . . back then.

Today the trends have changed and it's now cooler to dress as you, not as someone you want to be.

In my business, advertising, the old-school, cookie-cutter Don Draper look doesn't cut it anymore because it doesn't express the creativity people are looking for in their ad agencies these days.

Today if you want to be perceived as creative, you don't need to look like everybody else in the room to make them feel like you're one of them. In fact, you shouldn't try, because when it comes to your personal visuals, just as with your company's, looking different can actually be a plus. (To get all film-theory about it, it didn't work for Don Draper either. The whole point of that series was that Don didn't feel comfortable with who he really was, and his tight-fitting suits made him look fittingly uptight.)

But while the styles themselves have changed, the whole premise of dressing for success still makes sense on many levels, because we're all shallow about appearance—our own, and others'.

So how should you present yourself at an important event, interview, or meeting? These days, it depends on who you are—even beyond your job category or your industry.

"Who you are" literally means who *you* are, as a person—a party of one. If you were born in a hoodie, raised in a hoodie, love your hoodie, and have some sick hoodies, go ahead and wear the hoodie to that meeting, because you'll look like who you are. (Hey, it worked for Mark Zuckerberg.)

Simple clothes can show comfort and confidence, and the more confident and comfortable you are, the better you can perform—and the virtuous cycle continues. Just be sure it looks deliberate, put together, and not like you're wearing a hoodie because it was the first thing you found on the floor when you rolled out of bed. Even if your look is casual, you still need to acknowledge the fact that you are playing a part.

But the part is not a cameo. It's you, in the starring role. Own it, and success will follow.

REINVENT OR DIE!

WHEN STEVE JOBS RETURNED TO WORK AFTER the temporary remission of his cancer in 2007, he made a momentous announcement that effectively memorialized his influence upon the company he cofounded.

At the Macworld expo, he announced that Apple was dropping the word *computer* from the company name and becoming just plain Apple, Inc. "Of the Mac, iPod, Apple TV, and iPhone," Jobs said, "only one is a computer. So we're changing the name." It was super-clever because he was telling the world that Apple wasn't just a computer company but a lifestyle company. And as soon as you make your products part of the lifestyle of people, you've made it part of their life, which is to say something they can't live without.

This reinvention cemented Apple's future, making it at least temporarily the most expensive stock of all time.

Another company that recently reinvented itself is Under Armour, an athletic apparel company that made its fortune selling moisture-wicking T-shirts. But simply by acquiring three apps (to the tune of half a billion dollars) that track health, fitness, and nutrition, UnderArmour transformed themselves literally overnight into a digital sports company. Now they have the world's biggest network of apps for tracking health and fitness.

Those who adapt to change can eventually make change. Once you reach that level, adaptation is easy because you've not just predicted the future but created it.

DON'T TELL YOUR OWN STORY: MEDIA 1.0

I F YOU TELL YOUR OWN STORY TO POTENTIAL IN-
vestors, clients, partners, and customers, you'll just sound like a desperate self-promoter. Instead, pitch it to reporters. When they tell your story for you, you'll sound like a rock star.

When you talk about how good your company is, it's known as bragging. When a journalist talks about how good your company is, it's known as objective journalism, otherwise known as the truth ;). Kiip is known as a media darling, and the press we've received has been immensely valuable to us. It's put us in the hearts and minds of our clients, our investors, our peers, the public, and other media people.

We could not possibly have reached the level that we have without press coverage. If you're also an entrepreneur, or want to be, it's doubtful that your business and your brand—even if your brand is just you—can get where you want to go without the help of media.

And did I forget to mention that it's free—and worth far more than any expensive ad campaign?

The best thing about media is that it's the gift that keeps on giving. Once you get one person to tell your story, it tends to trigger a ripple effect, with one news outlet following the lead of another. I'm sure that in school your teachers taught you not to copy off someone else's paper. In journalism school, they teach you *how* to copy off someone else's paper—with just enough dressing to make it seem new.

I learned about the value of media relations at one of my earliest jobs, at 1-800-GOT-JUNK?, where my job was to make something as boring as junk removal into a palatable story. It taught me the art of angles, finding creative junk-related hooks I could use to pitch stories, whether it was Earth Day, the newest waste-removal laws, or the war that was being launched against the newly recognized problem of hoarding.

Then I moved to the Net-centered news aggregator Digg, which was the perfect place to learn how to interact with reporters. My job there started with trying to get reporters and news publication operations staff to integrate the Digg button into their websites, and telling them how they could make their content more Digg-able. Then I went straight to the heart of media relations: getting Digg into the news.

It was fun, with only one significant sacrifice: paying bar tabs before I was legally allowed to drink. Ironic, yes—but worth it to make friends with the cream of tech journalism.

Legal drinking age or not, I ended up spending time—a lot of time—in bars with a lot of reporters, talking about how great Digg was. Naturally, once they got some alcohol in them, I became much easier to tolerate. After a few drinks, I was actually perceived as cool—and after even a few more drinks, they accepted me into their tribe.

But kiip this in mind: while I am a salesman and proud of it, I'm not a manipulator or a bullshitter. If I can find a logical, true reason why people should buy what I'm selling, I milk it. But if I can't find a reason, I won't try to sell it to them. This philosophy extends to media as well. If I don't have a good story to pitch you, I won't come to you with garbage. I'm in business for the long haul, and when it comes to the long game, reputation is the most valuable asset I have.

Over time, I became good friends with a lot of reporters. Contrary to how they're often portrayed in the movies, they're actually not coldhearted opportunists (though the cinematic portrayal of their drinking habits, I learned, is generally true). They're in business for the long haul too, and they don't burn sources or make up shit just to get a headline. With few exceptions, they're serious, stand-up people.

So I treat them with respect, and I value their opinions, because they talk to everybody and know all kinds of things I don't. Sometimes it's like I'm interviewing them rather than vice versa. It's part of an organic exchange of information. It's also flattering to them. Part of the theater of journalism is that reporters are expected to constantly defer to their sources—as if the source is the oracle and the reporter is just the humble servant of the public, who's there to take notes. Reporters get tired of subsuming their own egos (which can be sizable, since they're people who chose a profession that's based on getting attention), so when you put them in the spotlight for a few minutes, they tend to love it. Just as with a lot of people who work behind the scenes, any show of respect is welcome.

I collected a lot of phone numbers working at Digg, and later Kiip, and did a lot of texting—most of it really casual. I just wanted journalists to know who I was, and that I enjoyed their contact. They moved around a lot in their careers—more than journalists did in the past, because journalism is still in a state of flux—but I stayed in touch with all of them and ended up building a number of really tight connections that have resulted in dozens of favorable stories that helped me gain amazing aware-ness for both my personal brand and my business.

The bottom line: You cannot take a start-up from zero to prosperity without knowing exactly how to optimize media relations.

Media is so important that I've got several more cheats on it. If you want to know all the stuff that took me all those expensive bar tabs to figure out, kiip reading!

MAKE BOLDNESS YOUR GENIUS: MEDIA 2.0

A S I SHOWED IN THE LAST CHEAT, YOU CAN stack the cards of media coverage in your favor if you start by making friends with journalists, or at least building relationships built on mutual trust and respect.

But don't expect these relationships to lead to automatic puff pieces on you or your company. That's not how the game is played. Reporters can't get away with writing gratuitous bullshit, and you shouldn't even want them to. Even if you do manage to convince someone to publish a love letter to your company, it will smell like bullshit to the reader. Audiences now are savvy, even to the level of cynicism. They've seen it all, and they don't want to see it again.

Knowing a journalist doesn't guarantee you automatic press coverage. It just gives you one less hoop of credibility to jump through in order to get it.

You can also help your chances by giving those reporters what they need to make headlines. Don't forget that whether the medium is print or online, at the end of the day what journalists are after are *eyeballs*—so the more you can give those reporters stories that will grab people's attention, the better off you are. How do you do this? Be bold. Be very bold.

Boldness is the veritable watchword of *The Cheat Code*. Burn this quote into your brain: "Boldness has genius, power, and magic in it." That quote is often attributed to Johann Wolfgang von Goethe—from 250 years ago—and it's like he was thinking of me when he wrote it. Be bold in your pitches to the media because that's the place to shout your glory to the rooftops. The least opportune time to be a shrinking violet is with the media. Journalists want to write about the companies that don't need attention, because they're already hot—and these companies tend to reject media to avoid overexposure. So the more you can provide those journalists with bold, fresh, valuable content that will help them earn those reader eyeballs, the more likely you are to get coverage. Another mini cheat is to let them know that you're giving them the scoop first—we all like to be the first person to know something, but reporters even more so, since they make their living that way.

That's ass-backward, but hey, so is much in business.

If the only thing you can give reporters is something that's self-serving, they'll tell you to buy an ad. Writers are smart people who've been played before, and if you don't deliver something that really is new or has some other good hook, you're dead meat.

So here's your homework: Think of a hook for your business, or for the business you'd like to start. You surely must have something unique, or you wouldn't be in that business or contemplating it. If it's unique, it's new—and that's all you need.

When you look for your hook, suspend your normal thought processes and don't think like you. Think like the writer you're giving it to. Put yourself in the writer's shoes. That's harder than it sounds, because the writer won't be thinking like the writer either. The writer will be thinking like the reader. So just think like the writer who is thinking like the reader . . . and it's a snap.

Your hook is probably hidden in plain sight. If you don't see it, you may just be too close to the whole thing and can't see the forest for the trees. Step back. Look again.

It's probably so simple you can say it in ten words. In fact, it needs to be simple. The world already has enough complexity. I can say mine in five: I sell advertising people like.

One final mini cheat: Crafting a hook is an art, so it's not a bad idea to hire a publicist. They're the true artists of communication, because they know how people think on all three sides of the triangle: They know how to think like you, they know how to think like the guy writing about you, and they know how to think like the reading public.

MAKE THE NEWS! MEDIA 3.0

ONCE YOU'VE BECOME FRIENDS—OR AT LEAST drinking buddies—with some journalists and figured out a hook to whet their appetites, now it's time to go fishing!

The most dependable media bait of all is news so new it hasn't even happened: an announcement. Better yet, a pending announcement.

Here's what you do: You drop a hint to some reporters that you've got something huge coming up. You don't hand them the whole thing; just provide enough detail to get them hooked.

You need to be especially careful to not say too much. You'll get much more value letting it play out over time. Also, the more information you give them, the more they have to find fault with (the media can find fault with anything; it's part of their job) and shoot down.

You really are doing your reporter friends a favor when you give them a sneak peek before their competition gets hold of it. Remember, writers and reporters (and especially business writers, who don't always have a steady stream of breaking news coming in) need scoops: "You heard it here first!" So if you imply that you'll give them something hot before anyone else hears about it, you've got not only their attention but also their sincere appreciation.

Do they know you're using them? Absolutely. Is that fine with them? Abso-fucking-lutely. Why wouldn't it be? It's a win-win situation.

When you first dangle the bait, do it in a low-key way. A quick text—something like, "Hey, we've got a cool new product launch coming up, I'd love to let u in on it"—is good, especially since you've probably already been texting them about other stuff, such as "Nice story yesterday" (if you aren't doing this, you should be).

If they call you or email you about it, make sure they know they're high on your list of initial contacts. Theirs doesn't have to be the only name on your list, especially if those names work in different venues: a newspaper, a magazine, a blog, a news site, a radio outlet, a TV network. If you're leaking a big announcement, you want to make sure you have someone from each of these media covered. And they'll expect you to.

When you've got a few people stirred up, toss out your bait as an email. It should offer just the bare-bones gist of it. For example: "I've got a new app for real estate professionals," or "I've got something that Airbnb will never see coming." When I first launched Kiip, it was "I've got a new form of advertising that's not intrusive that people actually want." More recently it was "We're about ready to enter into a major deal with MasterCard."

The way to position it is like this: "This email is kind of a heads-up that something big is happening, and I want to hop on the phone to share more color." I love the phrase "share more color" because it's vague enough to pique their curiosity and promises enough to give them a reasonable excuse to spend time with you on the phone.

You want to milk the story as much as possible; stretch it out over multiple emails to build suspense. If the emails are short, they might reply with something like, "I need more details," so you tell them you'll hop on the phone with them.

With any luck, the reporter will print or post something like tech media whale Michael Arrington did in *TechCrunch* when I told him about the birth of Kiip shortly before it happened. He wrote, "Wong may be the youngest entrepreneur to raise venture capital—Mark Zuckerberg was just 20 when he raised early money for Facebook. ... We've got our crack team of research interns looking into exactly who holds the record as the youngest entrepreneur to have raised a proper venture round. Kiip.me is still a few months away from launching. Stay tuned."

In just a few paragraphs—which didn't mention anything other than an impending announcement—Arrington made my life a whole lot better than it had been the day before. All this was even before we announced that Kiip was in business. And when we did, guess who was one of the first reporters to get that scoop?

I did the same basic thing much more recently, when Kiip made a huge deal with MasterCard. Want to hear about it?

Stay tuned.

MAKE OTHER PEOPLE FEEL SMART

THE SMARTEST PERSON IN THE ROOM IS USU-ally the person who says, "You guys are all so smart."

The smartest people surround themselves with other smart people.

You probably work with and socialize with intelligent people. There are plenty of people in the world who don't have much imagination or wit, but if you're reading this book, you probably don't deal with too many of them in your business or social life. After all, the smartest people surround themselves with other smart people—and I know you are one of them.

But smart people don't tell other people that they're smart just to kiss their ass. They do it to get through to them. It's one of the best ways to get someone who's intelligent on your wavelength.

Unfortunately, many people expend energy trying to prove to others how smart they themselves are. But that usually backfires, because it makes whatever you say look like a cry for respect or approval, which is just another form of being needy. People, especially in business, don't want to fulfill your needs—they want you to fulfill theirs.

I often run into people who are obsessed with telling me all about their brilliant technology—not just what it does but the back end, how it's made. They're obviously smart enough to create something, but I already knew that when I started talking to them. So even when their technology is ridiculously amazing, if it's hard for me or some other non-engineer to understand, it's not worth explaining. We'll just end up feeling stupid, which is the opposite of what you want.

Making people feel smart is one element of how Apple launches new products, like their new Apple Watch. On their product's new site, they put a lot of effort into showing beautifully produced videos of the Apple Watch's raw materials—mostly the metals: aluminum, gold, and stainless steel. The videos are about two minutes long, and tell you a bit about the science that went into the metals that compose the Apple Watch. The videos are interesting and informative, without talking down to people. Now, most people aren't metallurgists, or even remotely versed in how to create different alloys. But the fact that you can kind of understand it makes you feel like: "Wow, they put so much effort into the freaking metal that I'm buying this! It's way worth all this money!"

The point is that Apple invariably breaks down complex ideas in a comprehensible way that makes the audience feel smarter. Apple's site says, for example, that the Apple Watch "keeps time within 50 milliseconds of the definitive global time standard." There's not a word in that claim that you don't understand, so even though you may not really know what the "definitive global time standard" is, you kind of, sort of feel like you do. You know what "definitive" means, and you know what "global," "time," and "standard" mean. So just put them together, right?

I was spending time with my head of engineering recently and we were breaking down all the products that Kiip has. I started talking about one of the things a product can do, and he's like: "That's not actually what it does." But what it really did do was super-close to what I was saying, so I go, "Yeah, but that's the thing that people will grab on to, and listen to, and understand. And that understanding will make them feel smart."

When you use a term like "machine learning," for example, people know the meanings of "machine" and "learning," so it sounds smart to them, and they feel like they're smart just to understand it. It doesn't matter that machine learning doesn't actually involve a machine that can learn. It's actually just a series of formulas that inform your calculations. But describing it as "machine learning" makes it sound so addictingly smart.

Everybody in the world wants to be smart. People open up to you when they think you recognize and respect their intelligence. If you try too hard by making things complicated—or, worse, by talking down to someone—you'll fail. But if you give people just enough information to feel like they understand something complicated or hard, they'll almost instantly be on your team. You agree with that, don't you? You must. You're so smart.

GET TO THE POINT!

IF YOU'RE IN THE BUSINESS WORLD, ONE THING IS inevitable: you're going to encounter a lot of bullshit. When people start beating around the bush—giving you the vague "context," offering unconvincing "illustrations," and burying you in all kinds of meaningless "important details"—you've got to wonder: Do they have a point?

After all, if they had a good point, why wouldn't they just get to it? If it's such a good point, why does it need so much window dressing?

If you hear someone saying "Long story short . . . ," it's not short enough. You should live by that maxim as well. Leave the verbiage, redundancy, and time-wasting to the bureaucrats, the idiots, and the insecure.

The reduction of ideas to their ultimate core is a great bullshit-meter. Simplicity reveals, while complexity conceals.

That's true about everything from products to philosophies. Winston Churchill, who won a Nobel Prize for literature, said, "The short words are the best, and the old words when short are the best of all."

One of the best things about Kiip is that I can explain the

whole concept in about a sentence: "With Kiip, advertisers reward people with free things during moments of achievement on apps and games."

Most of the pages on our site only have about a hundred words on them. We're not trying to outsmart anybody. We don't have to. What we have to offer speaks for itself.

When people look at our site, or listen to us talk, or read our emails, they don't think we're trying to impress them—and that's impressive.

Time is money. Don't waste mine. If you've got something to say, say it. If you don't, go back to the drawing board, work up something that's good, and come back. I'll always listen to a good idea—I just don't want to waste my life listening to all the bullshit that comes before it.

Good ideas come in short sentences.

Good ideas are easy to explain because they're ideas people already know, even if they haven't heard them.

Concise is good.

Long-winded is bad.

How's that for getting to the point?

KIIP YOUR MIND WIDE OPEN

STEVE JOBS'S LAST WORDS WERE: "OH WOW! OH wow! Oh wow!"

His sister, who was at his bedside, described the words as a reflection of Jobs's "capacity for wonderment, the artist's belief in the ideal, and the still more beautiful later."

It's impossible to know what Jobs really meant or was experiencing. But it's hard not to feel as if, right there on his deathbed, he was seeing something new.

The point about Steve Jobs's last words is what they reveal about his capacity for wonderment. It was almost as if he simply was at one more of the hundreds of meetings at Apple when someone had described the possibility of creating something that not only didn't exist yet but also had never even been dreamed of until that point.

The most incredible of all dreams are those flights of imagination in which someone sees what others should have seen long ago. The nature of Jobs's genius was that he could see what was hiding in plain sight.

How did he do it? He kept his mind wide open. Jobs was a master of the brilliant question that is sometimes considered the dumb question. Does something exist, or not? *Can* something exist, or not? Break it down.

The entirety of the Western philosophy of learning kicked off about twenty-five hundred years ago with Socrates, whose Socratic method revolved around simply asking questions.

In the East, the same essential style of learning was based on the Zen Buddhist concept called *shoshin*, which means "beginner's mind." That kind of mind has no preconceptions, and as a result, it can see all kinds of possibilities, while the experts only see the few that already exist.

Jobs, fascinated by Zen, was famous for going into meetings like he was the dumbest guy in the room and asking people to explain stuff in words that cats and dogs could understand. A lot of the time the questions he asked weren't even precise, but just vague, general things—more like Rorschach inkblots of questions.

But they generally seemed to elicit smart answers, and the more intently Jobs listened, the smarter the answers became. Then he'd ask something like, "Can you rephrase that?" Then he'd finish with, "Why?" By the end of it, Jobs had often dug up a nugget that helped take the company in some new and previously unimagined direction.

Where will his successor take it from here?

That's a good question. I'll have to think about it. I try to kiip an open mind. If your mind is open, you can find great ideas in all kinds of unexpected places.

KIIP MOVING

A S I WRITE THIS I'M SETTLING INTO MY SEAT AND getting some work done as we lift over Rome en route back to San Francisco, trying not to make too much eye contact with the guy next to me, because it's a long flight and I don't want to get roped into a lengthy conversation. It's true, you can meet a lot of interesting and influential people on planes, and sometimes it leads to good opportunities or new knowledge. But I find it's best to make contact late in the flight, because you can still connect without wasting time on hours of chitchat that you're really not interested in.

I hate wasting anything, and time is high on the list.

I hate wasting time so much that on the flight over, I got pissed at myself for even heading for Rome because I've already been there, and what I love most about traveling is seeing new places. Every place in the world is its own university, offering you a new view of life with its kinesthetic kaleidoscope of sights, smells, feelings, and tastes, and I try to cram in as much of that experience as possible.

So I was annoyed not only because I was going somewhere I'd already been but also because I was coming for just one event, without my usual packed agenda, so it felt as though my time was being doubly wasted.

The event was a big one, though: the Festival of Media Global, where the senior execs from the world's biggest brands get together with the greatest ad and marketing people in the world. And while I didn't have any formal meetings planned, my gig there was keynote speaker, so it was definitely a worthwhile investment of time.

But I was still annoyed by going to only one place to do one job. That's just my personality.

I know that might sound weird, but I love to just go, go, go, and keep going. It makes me feel super-alive and ultra-productive. When you're on the go, you never know what will happen—and sometimes the only reason something happens is because you're on the go.

So in an effort to make the most out of every second of my trip, on my flight out of New York, I hit Google Maps and saw that the closest big city to Rome was Florence, or Firenze—birthplace of the Renaissance! Since my goal in life is to be a Renaissance man, I knew I couldn't go wrong in Firenze.

The trip alone was sick. We blasted out of Rome on Rail Europe at 220 miles an hour, and for an hour and eighteen minutes I devoured the luscious if speed-blurred visuals of Tuscany flashing past the window like a surreal Van Gogh painting. Then—boom!—we were there! My kind of train ride.

Florence has fabulous museums (and you probably guessed that I love museums, because they're like a high-speed rail hop through history), so I tore through them for six straight hours, taking a jillion photos, topped by an up-close experience with Michelangelo's *David*. When it's right in your face, it's like you're doing more than just looking at it. It's truly a ridiculous work of art. In five hundred years nobody's done better sculpture, and being that close to it stamps an indelible lesson about excellence on your brain.

The next day I jumped on the first train out to Pisa, where the Leaning Tower was finally open after twelve years of restoration. It turns out what they say is true: Your whole body can feel the lean when you climb up it. And before I knew it, time was up. On to Roma.

Now, I go to huge international business events all the time—Cannes Lions, South by Southwest, you name it—but for a guy like me, the Festival of Media is like media nirvana. Every global heavy hitter in business and the media-buying business is there, because it's one of those things that isn't cheap to get to or attend, and that weeds out everybody but the decision makers.

So you tend to find yourself sitting down to lunch with people like the heads of media for HSBC, Fiat, and Reckitt Benckiser (makers of Lysol and so on). It was a conference awash with pure energy if I ever saw one.

I traded business cards and interesting information with countless people from around the world, and especially Europe—a hot, huge market for Kiip right now. We're now generating a lot more revenue from Europe than ever because of our recent campaigns for Coke and Coke Zero, so opportunities abound, and every conversation seems to lead to one.

Before I knew it, it was time for my speech—a feel-good message about the new era in which advertising isn't intrusive—and I took the stage to Pharrell Williams's song "Happy," the obvious opening score for a speech I called "Because I'm Happy: Capturing the Perfect Moment." I like to think it helped people feel happy about what they were doing and why they were there, and—as it always is when you connect with an audience—it felt like I was making a thousand friends at once.

Then it was on to the gala dinner, which stretched out to

about 4:30 in the morning. Meaning it was over early enough to go somewhere else and have another experience.

I'd never seen the Roman Colosseum, and what more perfect time is there for avoiding crowds than 4:30 a.m.? A few minutes in a taxi, and there I was.

It was amazing. It was so quiet you could almost hear the history of the place, with gladiators clanging swords and crowds roaring, even though there were no people in sight!

Well, there was one person. He was about a hundred yards from me. Another tireless sightseer, I figured. Or not. Then he started walking toward me. Moving faster. Faster. Too fast. Holy shit!

I had two choices: stick around and see what's up with this guy, who might turn out to be the most interesting person I'd met yet, or run like hell.

If I ran, I'd never know what the guy wanted. Maybe he was running toward me because he'd been at the Festival of Media, heard my speech, and wanted to do a deal. Or maybe he was a pickpocket, a recent escapee from a mental asylum, or a serial murderer.

I decided not to find out. I spun around and booked it down the street. He kept coming. Two blocks. Two and a half. I was panting. I still had a bottle of one of the finest wines in Italy in me, and he probably didn't. This would not work to my advantage.

Then he slowed, and finally stopped.

Not me. I kept moving.

As I've said, to keep moving is a wise strategy—in business, in life, and, as I learned that night, maybe in *saving* your life too.

DON'T OVERSHARE

I REMEMBER MY FIRST OLD-MAN MOMENT. IT WAS the kind of harbinger of late life you never forget—it marks the moment where you begin to stare down the barrel of the vast sweep of time that carries you, in our fast-forward era, all too quickly toward the somber, reflective epoch in life.

It happened at a concert, where, at the ripe age of twenty-two, I was suddenly the old dude who wasn't fixated on his phone.

In my defense as somebody who's still got a little youth left in him, it was at an Imagine Dragons concert, where the demographics skew toward seventeen-year-old girls. But still.

What was I doing there? To set the record straight, I was brought there by a girl. Who was older than seventeen, I should add.

But the point is, as I was listening to the band (which was actually good), I found myself in this sea of teenage girls Snapchatting every precious moment to their friends. What struck me was the disconnect between how the girls seemed to be experiencing the concert and the experience they were surely trying to convey to their friends. As far as I could tell, they seemed as bored and detached as newspaper reporters in old movies. But surely the photos they were sending to their friends were meant to show how much fun was being had. My attitude was like: "Girls, the friends you're sending this stuff to are probably enjoying the concert more than you! Wouldn't you enjoy the concert more if you weren't a total slave to Snapchatting photos to your friends?"

The moral of the story is: Get over the idea that you've got to share every darn thing you ever think or do with everyone you know, as well as the assumption that the more people you share something with the more popular you are. It exposes more of you than you really need to, and at the same time takes you out of the experience you are trying to live. Look at all the celebrities who shot themselves in the foot by oversharing every detail of their private lives.

Besides, it's totally counterproductive, because the more you put out there the faster people get tired of keeping up with it. In the attempt to seem important, your stuff gets so weak and tired that people think you've got nothing important to share.

Another downside to making yourself into an on-the-scene reporter is that you stop bothering to remember things and lose what could be some of your most precious memories.

I like to keep my best memories off-camera and as private as possible. It makes them more vivid. You remember the way it really was, rather than the way a photo or video makes it look.

Remembering what happened to you is a classic way to train your mind, and it doesn't dilute remembrances of things past with the static of digital interference. Seriously, I know people who go around thinking: "Did I see this on social media, or experience it myself? I dunno—it doesn't matter."

Yes, it does.

Real life matters, and so do the people you share it with.

So instead of constantly broadcasting your life, why don't you try living it?

DROP OUT OF DROPPING OUT!

HERE'S A BEDTIME STORY THAT COLLEGE KIDS tell themselves while they toss and turn at the thought of surviving another term: "Once upon a time, in a land of Fierce Competition, a little college boy named Bill Gates [you can sub-stitute Steve Jobs or Mark Zuckerberg] worked very hard, so that one day he could have a good job. But evil old professors who knew that he was destined to be the Prince of Money burdened him with dull ideas that hurt his big brain very, very much. One day he broke free, ran far from the School of Dullards, and joined a merry group of brave escapees from college who had magical ideas: Michael Dell, David Karp, Kevin Rose, Larry Ellison, Jack Dorsey, and Paul Allen, to name a few. They had great fun, and soon ruled the entire kingdom—which they renamed DropOut Land, in honor of the proven fact of history that every billionaire dropped out of college—and lived happily ever after. With a hot girl. And a Gulfstream G500. The End. No, two hot girls, and a yacht with a helipad, like Larry Ellison's. The End."

Given that I work in tech, people all around me have bought into this fairy tale, and it's just hilarious when you see them try to bring it to the real world. They're like, "Whoa, dude, I just dropped out of college and now I've got this massive freedom, so I'm gonna be an entrepreneur, because that's cool—and if I don't like it, I'm gonna jump ship and head straight for the hot new thing!"

It's the curse of my generation. We didn't invent bailing, but we sure as hell made an art form of it.

I often have to warn people about the dangers of not seeing things through. I think that one of the biggest cheats in life is proving that you have the integrity to finish what you started. That's the one thing that makes you the type of person other people will rely on, and come to, when they really need something. The dropout ethic has been legitimized to such a degree that there are now two essential approaches to entrepreneurship. In one, the entrepreneur builds his idea into a company for the primary purpose of selling it. That's considered a viable business model, and I'm not saying people haven't made money from it—but think about this: Is making money the be-all and end-all of life?

Plus, do you really want to be known as the guy who took the money and ran from your first start-up?

What about the people who helped you build the company and who are going to get axed by the new management? It's unlikely that they'll ever want to do business with you again. And what about your own reputation as somebody who doesn't know how to take something to the next level, somebody who's always chasing the hot new thing, no matter whom he has to run over to catch it?

And plus, what if there *is* no hot new thing? What if you're burned out and washed up by thirty?

What if the $10 million you made on the sale of your start-up taxes down to $5 million, then drops to $4 million after you piss away about a million of it on living the life of the young rich?

What do you do when it drops to $2 million after you dump your own money into something that flops, because nobody else believes you'll see it through (and they're right)? What if you realize you're all out of killer ideas, and settle down with a pretty nice house, an okay car, and enough left over to—based on returning the standard 5 percent in the market, after taxes—give you an income of $40,000 a year?

Is that the dream you dreamed when you lulled yourself to sleep in college with fairy tales of being a power dropout?

Then there's the other approach to entrepreneurship, the one I followed. First you finish school, where you learn how to think critically, engage socially, and plan for your future—rationally. Then, once you get the idea of your life, you have the tools to turn it into a dream so real you can hold it in your hands, and make other people see it too. You love the idea almost as much as you might someday love a wife or child, and the work you do on it feels more like play, as other people are drawn to it, and drawn to you. Some are investors. Others are customers. Doesn't matter, because they all feel like family to you.

You and your band of brothers and sisters create something that makes life better right away, and it spreads so effortlessly that it seems harder to keep it small than make it big.

As your company grows, your equity grows. Money always stays real, and greed is never something that keeps you up at night. You stay the course, not out of a sense of guilt, responsibility, or inertia, but because you love what you do so much that cutting and running never once even enters your thought process.

People see you as a person who is true to his ideas, true to his word, and true to the people around him. Your embrace of loyalty as an ethic becomes as natural as your love of your idea, and is seen as a central part of your identity.

Your life makes sense.

You wake up one day in a land of Fierce Competition, which you rule kindly but firmly, with the bluebirds singing, and weaving ribbons together as they fly (a lot like in *Cinderella*, but better, because they're designing your new logo), as your princess calls out, "Prince of Money! Breakfast is ready!"

You pinch yourself. It leaves an ugly bruise. Must be real life.

COFFEE WITH BRIAN!

ABOUT FIVE HUNDRED TIMES A YEAR, SOME-body says to me, "I'd love to have coffee with you for about fifteen minutes, and pick your brain."

As a rule, these people are starting to nurse an idea into a business, or they're entrepreneurs whose project has stalled.

I usually tell them, "Sorry, but that would be just another fifteen minutes taken away from you actually doing something."

Some people get this. For them, it's the best possible advice I can offer.

Some people don't get it at all. For them, I have no advice that will help.

I would continue, but I've made my point. It would be just another fifteen minutes taken away from me actually doing something.

Or you actually doing something.

That's all for today, on *Coffee with Brian*!

DON'T GET DRUNK AT WORK

"DUH" WOULD BE A REASONABLE RESPONSE TO that—until you think it through.

You may think, "The last time I got drunk at the office was . . . never." That's a start. But please note that the title of this cheat is not "Don't Get Drunk at the Office." It's "Don't Get Drunk at Work." And if you're an entrepreneur or in any kind of management position, you know that a lot of work gets done outside the office. A great deal of that work is critically important, because it typically presents a good opportunity to get to know someone above your pay grade, in a relaxed setting, unconstrained by the barriers of hierarchy, rank, or job title. A chance to get drunk with the boss: That's a great opportunity, right? Wrong.

The *Mad Men* days of three-martini lunches are not the modus operandi of the new economy. Lunch, though, is not the danger zone. That hour arrives at 5:00 p.m., with "a" drink after work with a business contact, colleague, or, worse, a superior. And it hits high gear at every networking event or office party you've ever been to.

I've been to hundreds of those parties—maybe thousands— and many of the people I met there became important business associates. Realistically, if you're not meeting important people at these parties, you're going to the wrong parties.

The social myth we've concocted is that at a party, everybody gets a free pass on decorum—especially if you've got a glass in your hand. It's a cherished myth, because it can be hard not to be nervous at parties. You might not know anyone, and the atmosphere is usually artificial—one of bravado mingled with gaiety—generally because most people are pretending it's just a party when it's really work.

After you've tossed back a few, it's easy to feel like you got instantly funnier and cooler—and maybe you did. But that's usually not how it comes across. If you're acting even a little tipsy, you're undercutting your intellect, your emotional intelligence, and your gravitas.

If you're acting drunk, you're just a clown.

The best people in business don't do that to themselves. That doesn't mean they're stodgy or puritanical. It means they know when, where, and with whom to party.

The same principle goes double for company office parties. Think about it: These are the people whose own livelihoods depend to some degree on your good judgment and character. Do you really want them to see you flirting inappropriately with the secretary or falling off a bar stool?

My just-say-no stance goes quadruple for drugs, even if you live in Colorado. For every person who thinks it's cool that you smoke weed—even if it is legal—there will be someone else who thinks you're just another slacker druggie.

Still, it can be awkward to look like the only Puritan in the crowd, so it's usually smart to have a drink in your hand. It makes you seem warmer and more relaxed, and it keeps serious drinkers from feeling judged.

It's also smart to actually drink from it. Sometimes just having something to do with your hands—like sip a drink—can put you more at ease. Just try to keep the actual booze in it to a bare minimum. Ask the bartender for a nonalcoholic cocktail. Ask for tons of ice. Cut it with water. Just nurse it.

The unexpected irony: You'll feel more relaxed and comfortable, because you're at the top of your game mentally. You'll be funnier, sound smarter, and look more together. That's what your colleagues want from you. If they want silly, they'll watch reality TV. Or they'll get silly drunk on their own time, at home. And that's totally fine. Just don't do it at work.

KNOW WHEN TO LET GO

IN EVERY ENTREPRENEUR'S LIFE, THERE'S A TIME to let go—of a project, an idea, or even a company. But how do you know when that time has arrived? Some people let go when the money's gone. Bad idea. Too late. You should have seen it coming.

Some people let go when their product doesn't work immediately. Bad idea. Too early. If it's a good product, based on a great idea, a few years later somebody will probably finish what you started and make a bazillion dollars.

Kodak invented the digital camera in 1975 but did virtually nothing with it, because they made most of their profits selling film. So they abandoned it, and eventually went bankrupt. They clawed their way back—more or less—but today they're not even in the photo business anymore; they mostly make commercial printers. Too bad, because if they'd stuck with it, they could have made it huge in the era of computers and mobile devices, the way some of their competitors did.

Imagine how the poor folks at Kodak who created digital photography felt having the rug pulled out from under them by their corporate overlords who saw no future in digital, and watching other companies explode with success a decade later, when the digital revolution erupted.

Some people who launch start-ups let go when they can find somebody to take over and buy them out. That's okay if you're ready to wash your hands of it and do something different. That's not for me, though. I love my company. I love the idea, the people, the impact, and the way we're manifesting it and growing it, month after month and year after year.

That doesn't mean the day will never come. Things change, and change has its own demands. Knowing exactly when to let go boils down to perfect timing, and timing is usually a gut feeling.

It's super-important to develop your knack for timing before you let go of something. If you don't hone those skills, you won't recognize the right time.

You learn timing in every phase of a project or business. Your lessons come one at a time: knowing when to start something, when to add to staff, when to accelerate, when to scale back, when to take risks, and when to pull your time and money away from risks.

The hardest single element of timing is learning to control your thoughts, perceptions, and actions during a pivotal moment. It doesn't matter if the moment is negative, like dealing with a financial setback or the loss of a key employee, or positive, like having an amazing opportunity. Either way, you'll notice that a lot of people around you are going into a frenzy and leaping before they look, or getting paralyzed, or running in circles. They become a victim of time instead of its master.

When cataclysm occurs, it can be tempting to cut and run—out of fear, out of excitement, or out of sheer panic. Resist this urge. Instead, stay focused. Channel the energy away from freaking out and toward analyzing the potentials. See that every major decision is just another fork in the road.

People who let themselves fall into the fast-forward mode—which feels kind of good, because it burns off nervous energy—end up focusing on obstacles: either obstacles to success or obstacles that threaten them with failure.

The key here is to reinterpret the obstacle. If you think of an obstacle as an obstacle, then it is a fucking obstacle. Chill, and look for the opportunities that surround every obstacle. Once you gear your gut to that way of thinking, you'll automatically know when to do what. By then, if the smart thing is to let go, you'll let go. If it's not, you'll hang on.

If I'm making it sound easy, it's because it is, once you get the hang of it. Life really isn't all that hard.

What makes it seem so hard? We do. It's all in our heads.

If you can control yourself during those times when chaos surrounds you, you'll slowly learn to develop the knack for sensing when it's time to step out of the ring and when it's time to stay in the fight.

FIND THE RIGHT FIT—AND *BE* THE RIGHT FIT

ONCE YOU KNOW YOUR SUPERPOWER, A PRImary goal is to find complementary superpowers in other people. When you find those people, make them part of your network, even if there's no business you can do with them at the moment. As always, the whole is always vastly better than the sum of its parts.

A classic example in any tech scenario is the symbiosis between the marketer and the creator or engineer. I've told many techies that we complement each other perfectly because I'm good at bringing things to market—branding, communicating, and getting people excited—and they're great at technology. That's such a specific compliment that people never mistake it for idle flattery. (Digression, and the randomest micro-cheat of the day: To remember the correct spelling of "compliment" and "complement," use the mnemonic device "*I l*i*ke to compli*ment people." Sorry to say, but your teacher was right—spelling counts. So does neatness.)

The same power of complements (not compliments) applies to the businesses you choose to work with. I can go to Coca Cola and tell them, "You guys are great at mass advertising, but weak in one spot—personalized, targeted advertising—and I've got the company that can cover that."

Here's another example. Automakers make some great cars, but they're not great at audio, so they go exclusively with audio companies like Bose or JBL to power their stereos. Each type of company plays to their appropriate complementary strength.

But you can't find the right fit—in an employee, business partner, or anything else—if you're not the right fit for someone else. It's a two-way street. You've got to hold up your end. If you're not excellent at something, don't expect to attract people who are.

Be warned: It's not valuable to achieve excellence unless your function is truly differentiated. That's what makes you the most indispensable. It's far better to be a great car designer than a great car mechanic. Why? Because there aren't a whole lot of people who know how to design a car, but there are tons of mechanics.

Bottom line: Know what you're not good at, and find someone who is.

AVOID EYE CONTACT

PEOPLE TEND TO THINK THAT MAKING THE MAXImum amount of eye contact is a key to trust. It's not.

There is truth in the old saying that the eyes are the window to the soul. But how comfortable are you when you find somebody looking through your window and into your deepest and most private thoughts, fears, and emotions?

It's not always a welcome intrusion. That's the thing to remember about eye contact.

If you're in a business meeting with someone, don't sit directly across from them—sit at least slightly perpendicular. That way, your line of sight is not always straight at them, and you won't have to stare into each other's souls the whole time—or worse, risk looking evasive, shy, or dismissive by blatantly avoiding eye contact. It's human nature for people to stare off into space when they're concentrating on something, and if you're off to one side, you can do that more comfortably.

Some people are less comfortable with eye contact than others, and we tend to assume that's because they're a little more emotionally withdrawn, but that's not always the case. All good businesspeople are good actors, and sometimes acting shy is just part of the act. Maybe they're playing hard to get, or trying to draw you into their own sphere. There's no way to be sure, so don't presume too much.

When somebody acts shy, displaying the body language of reticence—including a soft tone, a protective stance, and minimal eye contact—some people try to compensate for the other person's introversion by acting more extroverted and applying more eye contact. It doesn't work. It usually makes people even more hesitant to look at you—either because they're genuinely shy and don't want to be stared at, or because they're playing you.

People sometimes also do the opposite and try to mimic the other person's avoidance of eye contact. That's not good either. It can just add to the awkwardness.

Another mistake people make is trying to be a hotshot interpreter of body language. If they see you looking down and to the left, they assume you're lying—usually because they've spent almost fifteen minutes on the Internet learning about nonverbal cues and saw that written on some random website. If they'd spent twenty minutes, however, they'd know that there are all kinds of other possible explanations.

The best strategy is to avoid the gamesmanship and focus on the desired agenda of clear, friendly communication. If you do, you'll look people straight in the eye when it's appropriate, and you won't when it's not.

In business, if you're looking to make a fair deal with somebody—one that's going to work equally as well for them as you, in the interests of a continued business relationship and common decency—just look at people as if they're people.

That's how we all want to be looked at, isn't it?

MIND YOUR MANNERS

SUCCESSFUL PEOPLE—ESPECIALLY YOUNG PEO-
ple—need to know two things about manners: (1) they're
very important, and (2) the definition of "good manners" varies
tremendously from group to group, country to country, and person to person.

Young people sometimes dismiss manners as some inconse-
quential relic of a stodgy, stratified culture of gentility that is fad-
ing fast. Big mistake. Manners evolve as quickly as technology,
and matter to everyone—just as much today as in the past.

In fact, they are as important to young people as to older people, oftentimes even more so. The problem many young people
have is just not knowing what constitutes good manners.

For example, if you're doing business with somebody in Asia,
you'll almost never hear a flat-out no in response to a question
or request because it's considered rude. If you ask them if they
can deliver something by Friday, they will say, "We can try."
That doesn't mean it will arrive Friday. It means they were being
polite.

If you want a straight answer, ask in a way that doesn't require
a yes or a no. They'll tell you the truth, and you'll get the answer

you need. The point is that culture is everything when it comes to manners. And culture doesn't have to be tied to nationality or country of origin either.

For example, in today's modern workplace, where so many millennials now work right alongside baby boomers thirty or even forty years their senior, there are huge generational differences when it comes to manners. For example, a young businessperson might avoid striking up a conversation with an older, established executive if they just happen to pass them in the hallway because they think the older person would consider them presumptuous or even rude. They think they need an introduction, and are then supposed to be very kiss-ass and make small talk. Wrong. That attitude comes from watching too many old movies and not paying attention to the evolution of manners.

Important business executives know the only reason you're approaching them is because you want something. They don't want to play buddy-buddy, and they don't need you to tell them that you're a big fan. They want to know what you're after. So tell them. Fast. Get straight to the point. If you can't get to the point in the time it takes to walk with them from an elevator to an office, you're being the rude one.

The principle of straightforwardness also applies, oddly, to older people trying to connect to people who are very young. Remember that today's millennials grew up in a 140-character era, in which an emoticon is considered an entire unit of communication. If you want their attention and respect, don't email them an essay, or even phone them. Text them. Then you'll be talking their language.

The point: Be on somebody's wavelength. Respect their culture, just as you would the Asian businessperson's. That's good manners.

A key element of this is staying current with what's in among various subcultures. If you're talking to millennials, you need to know what *Game of Thrones* is. You don't have to like it, or even watch it, but if you act like you've never heard of it, you run the risk of seeming irrelevant and out of the loop—or, worse, aloof or disinterested. I'm too young to know why I should respect, let's say, Aretha Franklin, but I'm polite enough to keep that opinion to myself when I'm talking to a baby boomer. By the same token, I might not give a hoot about what some politician said last week, but if I'm doing business with someone passionate about politics, I would never act like it doesn't matter. That would be like telling the person I'm doing business with that they don't matter, something that's universally rude in any culture.

And speaking of universally rude, I would never go into a significant meeting of any kind without putting my phone on Do Not Disturb. I know that if I even *glance* at my phone during a meeting, there will be certain people who think I'm a self-absorbed millennial airhead.

One question I frequently get from people when I talk about the topic of manners relates to hugging in the workplace. Is it a polite show of warmth and affection, or a rude and inappropriate intrusion on another's personal space? The answer is that it depends, but when in doubt, take the other person's lead, especially if the other person is of the opposite gender. For example, I would avoid hugging a female executive unless she clearly initiated it.

Another potential minefield for manners: punctuality. In certain cultures it's rude to be late; in other cultures it's more polite to be late than early. For example, I would never arrive at a business meeting in New York late, but I would never arrive at a business meeting in Jakarta on time.

When it comes to minding your manners, keep your eyes and ears open and try to be respectful of every person that you meet. Try to get to know them. Try to see things from their perspective. And always say please and thank you—that's just universally polite everywhere.

One last universal truth: No one on earth is ever offended by an apology. So if you do offend someone inadvertently, as a result of not understanding their cultural norms around manners, apologize immediately. Please, thank you, and I'm sorry are the heart and soul of all manners, in any culture.

BE IGNORANT

THEY SAY THAT IGNORANCE IS BLISS, AND NO-where is this a truer statement than in the world of entrepreneurship and business. The bliss of ignorance frees you from the fear of failure, the fear of disappointment, and even the full knowledge of how hard the road ahead actually is.

When I first went looking for investors, shortly after the crash of 2008, I was only marginally aware that everybody was scared shitless and didn't want to risk what they had left—and certainly not on a nineteen-year-old boy who thought he could make people love advertising.

I'm not saying that my naiveté was the only reason I landed my first investor, but it helped.

Ironically, ignorance can breed confidence. When you're ignorant of your idea's flaws and potential pitfalls, you can look people in the eye and convince them that you know what you're doing. "The market crashed? People are defaulting? Banks are teetering? Never mind that! I've got the cure! Yes, our company is completely different—but that's good! Are you in or out?"

Sometimes it helps to be just ignorant enough to have more

Sometimes it helps to be just ignorant enough to have more faith in yourself than in the people who don't think you're worth the risk. After all, I knew me far better than I knew them. So it made perfect sense at the time. Call me ignorant, but ... strangely, it still does.

KNOW WHO'S THE BOSS

A LONGTIME SILICON VALLEY EXECUTIVE once took me aside and told me something I'd never forget.

"Brian," he said, "how long have you been in the Valley?"

"About a year and a half," I said.

"How long do you think the investors have been here?"

"I don't know. Twenty, thirty years?"

"Exactly. And how long have the lawyers and bankers been around? Same time—twenty or thirty years. Everybody that you're talking to about investing has been here longer than you. So what makes you think you are unique?"

I didn't have an immediate answer.

"The entrepreneurs," he said, "get shuffled through this conveyor belt, and as they come and go, the fixtures of the Valley—the investors, bankers, and lawyers—all remain."

He was absolutely right. Entrepreneurs like me are a vital part of the start-up economy, but we're just one part, and for that economy to thrive, we need to work with the people who built it, and respect their authority.

You need to know whom you're working for.

If you're an entrepreneur who wants to stay in the game, you essentially report to your investors. Even though I'm the CEO of Kiip, I still have several bosses: my investors, some of whom are on our board of directors. They expect some kind of return on their money, and it's my job to satisfy them.

At about the same time I had the aforementioned conversation with the executive, somebody else who knew the Valley well asked me another powerful rhetorical question: "Brian, do you serve your investors, or do your investors serve you?"

He got to his point quickly. "They should serve you. They didn't bring you in. *You* brought *them* in. They don't run the company. *You* do. They didn't have the idea. *You* did."

It sounded like two opposite perspectives.

Now I know they're both right.

You are working for your investors, and your investors are working for you.

The moment you accept that both of these ideas are true, you're ready to make money.

You won't need to be nervous about losing any particular investor, because you'll know that your investors need you as much as you need them.

You won't need to feel alone, because your investor wants you to succeed as much as you do.

You won't need to feel in over your head, because you always have immediate access to experienced, smart people.

You won't need to feel controlled or constrained, because they gave you their money to be the boss, not just a figurehead or conduit to their own agenda.

You won't need to feel insecure within your industry, because your investors gave you the most meaningful token of legitimacy: their money.

Each of these advantages is monumental, and they're not oppositional at all, but completely symbiotic.

One of our first investors, Paige Craig, is somebody who can tell you more about real-life, real-time business over lunch than some business professors or McKinsey consultants could tell you in a year. He's an ex-Marine who maxed out his credit cards and went to the war zones of Iraq, posing as a reporter, in order to meet the officials who would let him launch a company with the goal of trying to win over the Iraqi people with positive TV ads instead of force. He landed contracts, scaled his company, and was so successful that he retired in his mid-thirties and became an angel investor. Now he's known in L.A. as the "Mayor of Silicon Beach."

Shortly after I met Paige, he literally wrote me a blank check and told me we'd work out the details later.

What do you learn from that? The power of trust. Instinct. Balls.

As one of our earliest investors, he should be pretty happy about his return so far. So to come back to the original question, who is the boss in the relationship?

Answer: We both are.

LOOK LIKE YOU KNOW WHAT YOU'RE DOING

EVEN SOME OF THE MOST IMPRESSIVE PEOPLE on the planet have no idea what they are doing half the time. They are proof that if you want to be successful, you don't need to always know what you're doing: You just need to look like you know what you're doing.

We all land in situations, sometimes every day, in which we wish we had a slightly better handle on exactly what we are doing. Just today I had a meeting with a guy who's doing a company based around beacon technology—sort of like GPS, only with extremely pinpoint locating abilities, like knowing when you're in a mall and just passed the Ralph Lauren store. It's super-cool. It's super-sophisticated. It's also not very easy to understand.

I got the nuts and bolts of it, but not the details—but I didn't want to look like I was in the kindergarten phase of it. So instead of asking really basic questions or admitting that I didn't fully get it, I asked him intelligent, generic questions about the industry, like: What's the hierarchy of the companies in it? How does he think beacon technology will play out in the future?

We had an interesting conversation. I kept his respect, and

I ended up learning some of the things he probably thought I already knew.

You may have seen this technique in action if a manager or exec has ever come into your meeting and said, "You all know what you're doing—I'm just here to learn." It's a pretty clever way of learning what you don't know without having to admit to what you don't know. But it has to be done with genuine sincerity, because if there's any hint that you're being condescending—like, mingling with the little people—they'll think you're full of shit and start letting you know how much you really do have to learn. I've seen managers do that with a sort of smug look on their face, and they got eaten alive.

The point is you don't need to know the answers, just the right questions to push the boundaries, learn what you don't know, and get the information you need to move the idea forward.

If you show that you *want* to know what you're doing, people will give you the benefit of the doubt and assume you do know, or soon will. Be overtly willing to learn and everything will fall into place.

GET A TRADEMARK HAIRCUT

EVER WONDERED WHY DICTATORS HAVE FANCY haircuts? They have them so that you'll remember them. Or, more precisely, so that you'll remember them for their cool hair—rather than, for example, for being tyrants or monsters. In other words, it's their branding.

Even if you don't aspire to world domination, in business it's very valuable to have a little trademark that will make you memorable, particularly in our information-saturated society. In fact, a trademark is one of the most memorable—and cost-free—ways to stand out and get noticed in a noisy world.

At Kiip, our trademark is that we constantly invoke our own brand signature with tag lines like "Kiip it real," "Kiip going," and "Kiip it up" (as I'm sure you've noticed, I've also done this throughout this book).

Even in emails, I always say something like "Kiip up the good work," and 90 percent of the recipients respond positively to it. (The other 10 percent just tease me about being a nerd.)

The mini-cheat is to trademark your brand by creating your own language-within-a-language. At Kiip, we don't create ads;

we offer rewards. We don't reach consumers when they're impressionable; we create moments of serendipity. This isn't just how we happen to talk. It's a vocabulary we've strategically adopted, that we've made our own.

The point of creating your own language is to present yourself as unique, as completely differentiated from your competitors. It signals to people, "Those guys are in one business, and we're in a better one. We're in our own category."

Another version of creating a signature language that I use is choosing a new, relatively uncommon word every month, and using it repeatedly. I use it with my own team, with customers, in speeches, in print, and on the air. For example, I did that with "serendipity," and as often happens, I soon started hearing people parrot the word back to me, as if it were their own. When that happens, you know you've tapped a powerful force for subliminal bonding.

Those same people might even start repeating the phrase, sending it into the culture in waves of concentric circles, because it sounds so addictingly smart and cool.

You too can create a language for your company, or even for your own personal brand. Religions do it. Celebrities do it. Smart businesses do it. Even dictators do it.

By the way, for the record, I am not a fan of dictators, and never will be—unless someday I become one myself. And even then, I promise to be a really nice one. That's my pledge to the people of Earth, and I intend to kiip it.

TAP INTO THE POWER OF EMAIL

JAKARTA, THE JEWEL OF JAVA, SITS IN A BAY ON the Java Sea where wooden schooners still dock. In this, the sixth-largest city in the world, you'll find a head-spinning kaleidoscope of cultures, flowers, mountains, and architecture designed to take your breath away.

I compiled so many vivid impressions of it from my last trip there that they dwarfed even the importance of the business I was there to do. I just wish I could remember them.

Jakarta's vast swirl of action is a black hole for the mind's storage of memories. It trapped impressions that probably won't revive until I revisit the city again. Jakarta gives new meaning to the phrase "too much."

Here's an example: When I told my driver how many meetings I had scheduled that day, he cried, "Mr. Wong, you have *six meetings today*? That is not quite *possible*!" Turns out in Jakarta you can have only *one* meeting per day, because you'll spend the rest of the day going to it and from it. Jakarta's traffic is the stuff of legend. Its streets make Manhattan's look like the empty alleys of a ghost town.

But I did have six meetings scheduled, with six of the most

important groups of people in my industry in that part of the world. How did I get those meetings? I got them largely through the grace of my abilities to send cold emails, and I'd be damned if I was going to miss any of them.

Emailing is one of the great powers of the new business culture, and it can make or break a career. Its ultimate power is the ability to unlock the doors to the world's most significant people before you've ever even shaken their hands.

First, you've got to have their email address, right? But nobody does. That's how they want it. But in truth, even the most elusive of important people aren't that hard to find. The quick and cheaty way is through sheer trial and error; write your letter to them, then address it to their most likely email address (i.e., JackSprat@VISA.com) with a blind CC (BCC) to as many possible permutations of the most likely address as possible: (i.e., Jack@VISA.com, Sprat@VISA.com, Jack.S@VISA.com, JS@VISA.com, JSCEO@VISA.com, etc.). Develop your own plug-in system to generate as many possible addresses as you can. Of course, only one will land, and that's the one you want. You'll know the ones that aren't working if they bounce back. Once you have the winning combo, most likely it'll work for a large portion of the employees for that company as well. You'll be shocked at how often this method works.

There are other methods of obtaining addresses, and they invariably require more guts than brains. They include simply calling their office and asking for it, reaching out to one of your journalist friends who might have it, going through the company's public relations office, buttonholing the important person him- or herself at some industry event, and so on. Use your imagination.

Here's another tip: Once you get the address, email that person on the weekend. That's when important people deal with their emails. Still, chances are good that he or she won't open it . . . the first time. By the third or even fifth time, your name will sound familiar. Or maybe they'll just be curious. Or maybe they'll open it looking for a way to unsubscribe from whoever or whatever you are. Either way, be shameless and persistent, but be respectful.

Try to put something in the subject line that they can't resist. Dropping a name (i.e., "Jack Sprat from VISA suggested I contact you, re: X") is a safe bet. It's often good to mention someone they want to learn more about, such as a competitor.

Another smart tactic takes a page from the military playbook: Attack from all sides. Send the email from different accounts. Surround them: Get to their VP, their COO, or their golf caddy—anybody.

Above all, remember that connections beget connections. When you know enough people in their industry, you will get through. If you don't know enough people in their industry to get through, maybe you don't deserve to. Be worthy of their attention before you ask for it.

If you can't get in the person's face, at least get in their universe. Make your name visible in as many places as possible that might be within their sphere. The more your name pops up on their Twitter feed, in Instagram comments, in LinkedIn likes and comments, and in general areas like a trade journal, a magazine article, or a list of speakers, the more brand recognition you'll have, and the more successful you'll be. They'll think, "I know that name from somewhere," and will be more likely to respond.

Also make sure that your email offers them something. If you want to get the attention of important people, always be offering. Never be asking. Nobody wants to give. Everybody wants to get. That's human nature. Finally, if your goal is to get in front of them, face-to-face, create a deadline for a time to meet. One of the best is "I'll be in your city, in your building, on this exact date—give me five minutes and I'll solve a specific problem that I know you have."

Every time I go to another city—which is practically every week—I send out ten to fifteen cold emails. The more I do it, the less need I have for cold emails, but that doesn't mean it's easy to see people just because you've already met. Sometimes that makes it harder, because they may think they've already gotten all you can offer.

But more often than not, if you've followed the tips in this cheat, at least a few of those people will be curious, or at least courteous enough to meet with you for a few minutes.

Which brings us back to Jakarta. Cold emailing is how I got an 8:30 a.m. meeting with the Indonesian head of digital marketing for the global conglomerate Interpublic Group, Rachna Sharma. We arrived at 10:00 a.m.—hence my driver's panic. Rachna graciously thanked me for my punctuality.

Over the course of that day, I met—to my shock—some of the most influential people in Southeast Asia. Another of my cold emails had led me to someone as important as Rachna in another company, a third led to another major player, and the rest of my meetings sprouted from those.

It's not like I'm part of the family now, but today these folks answer my emails, respond to my WhatsApp messages, and take me seriously—all thanks to a couple of cold emails.

This is the power of the new communication tools that we all have at our fingertips. We are in an era of unprecedented social mobility and connectedness—for those of us bold enough to use it.

Your access to this world is probably within fifty feet of you right now.

Say hello to this world. Send some emails.

USE EXCLAMATION POINTS

HELL YES, USE EXCLAMATION POINTS! THEY GET people's attention!

If you're trying to stand out and get noticed, there's no such thing as being too emphatic or energetic. I've recently started using the word "really" a lot. And when I say a lot, I mean that I've been using it *a lot*! I really, really like the word "really." Exclamation points add the same emphasis with just one character.

Maybe you grew up thinking exclamation points were gauche. Maybe you're basically a laid-back person. Maybe you're usually understated or sarcastic. Maybe sometimes you're tired. None of that has to show in your emails.

The beauty of emails is that with the combination of two magical keys, you can transform yourself into an energetic, enthusiastic, credulous, well-rested, and well-hydrated dynamo. SHIFT+1 spins your morning grogginess into entrepreneurial gold.

Sometimes you really, really need to be a walking, talking exclamation point. That applies when you're talking to users, the press, and your partners. They need your energy, and feed off it. You especially need to offer this energy to your investors—even if it's just by using exclamation points in your emails to them. Remember, they've given you money because they want you to burn brighter than they do, love what you're doing, and want to be the best in the world. If you could communicate all this with just a click on your keyboard, why wouldn't you do it?!?!

In the same way that a smile, a firm handshake, or a commanding "Hi!" can light up a halo over your head and affect how people see you, exclamation points carry outsize loads of information. In an instant, they can signal success, enthusiasm, confidence, and ability.

Don't worry about it not being cool. There are no style points deducted for enthusiasm. And no one gets ahead by being disaffected or aloof. Be cheesy. Gush.

Exclamation points are also a great way of pushing your point across! But first, you really, really need to have a strong point to make, and you need to be very clear about what it is. Emphasis offers clarity.

For example, when I say, "I think we should go with Designer #2," I might be saying anything—or nothing. I might mean that I think Designer #2 is the lesser of two evils. I might mean that I just can't remember Designer #1's name. I might mean that Designer #2's business card happens to be sitting at the top of the papers in my trash can, staring at me.

But if I say, "I really, really think we should go with Designer #2!!!" it can only mean one thing: Designer #2 is the best person for the job. No question. That cuts through the ambiguity, especially when you're delivering your message through the cold, often expressionless format of print.

And on top of all this, when you use a well-timed exclamation mark, you can even convince yourself of something you might be ambivalent about. It can change your mood—just like how science has found that when you smile, the physical activity of smiling actually has immediate, positive effects on mood and attitude.

Even if you're laid-back, understated, sarcastic, tired, or all of the above, using or seeing an exclamation mark can wake you up and get you out of bed.

One caveat: *use* the exclamation mark, but don't *abuse* the exclamation mark!!!! People don't like that, even when they're not sure why. But if you're waiting for me to tell you exactly how many exclamation points is too many, sorry, you're out of luck. Like porn, we all know it when we see it.

BE
A TRAILBLAZER

CONVENTIONAL WISDOM
IS DEAD. THERE ARE
BETTER WAYS TO GET
AHEAD—THESE CHEATS
WILL PUT YOU IN THE RIGHT
MIND-SET TO BE A LEADER
AMONG YOUR PEERS AND
YOUR INDUSTRY.

THERE'S NO SUBSTITUTE FOR BEING THERE

A S I WRITE THIS, I'M SITTING IN THE DRAB, STER-ile, could-be-anywhere airport lounge, getting these thoughts down while waiting for my flight from Taipei to Malaysia, where I'm speaking at an event this evening with members of the Malaysian government. Then I'll be taking the last flight out in the evening to Singapore, where I'll arrive on what (I think) will be Tuesday there, and stay until Wednesday. Then I'll head to Jakarta on Thursday, where I'll meet with some potential investors, and then take a six-hour red-eye flight to Shanghai. I love red-eye flights. I can sleep in the same time zone as the people I'm visiting, and get a full day's work done when I wake up.

The point is that while I may live in San Francisco, I work in the world—like, the whole world. The world is my office. Today, that's nothing special. Everybody experiences some degree of that these days, and if you don't—if you only see yourself as working in one small slice of the world—then you're probably only leveraging one small slice of the opportunities in the world as well.

But to fully understand the world, you have to get out and *be in* the world. You can't leverage the full range of opportunities out there in the world until you're thousands of miles from your comfort zone. Part of the reason I travel so much is just because I like to see the perspective of our business from the outside in. I like to seek opportunities and also let them find us. But in order for that to happen, you need to be out there—regardless of what your business is.

When I go to Singapore I'm going to see people that I haven't actually spent time with in two years, but we're going to catch up like old friends because we've kept in touch. They may not be necessarily relevant in that moment to what I'm doing with the company, but I am flying across the world to spend time with them because I know they'll have interesting perspectives that I'll learn from.

Smart people don't think about globalization anymore, because it's the default. If there's one thing that weaves together tens of millions of millennials, it's that with a tap of your finger you can send information around the world in a split second. It's something we grew up with that no generation ever before did.

As a result, many millennials—including me—consider themselves to be citizens of the world. This is particularly true in the technology industry, because the tech world is the very essence of a boundary-free environment. I'm the perfect example. I'm a Canadian citizen, with parents from Asia, who now lives in America, and I'm privileged to be able to travel very extensively. So to me, being in another country is more like being in another neighborhood. The world, not San Francisco, is home—and I feel at home almost everywhere.

But even though it's never been easier to keep in touch with people you know all over the world, whether through Facebook, Twitter, WhatsApp (a chat app very popular outside the United States that sends instant, cross-platform text, image, video, and audio messages anywhere in the world), or anything else, there's still no substitute for actually going somewhere and seeing the sights, hearing the sounds, and smelling the smells.

There's a saying among politicians: "Half of politics is just showing up." And that's true of business too. Realistically, it applies to just about every element of life that's governed by human connection, and it's never been more true than now, when so many people depend on virtual media.

It's easier, of course, to stay in the comfort of your own cocoon. And it's easy to rationalize staying at home by focusing on your e-relationships. Of course, there's no place like home. But that also means there's nothing like being away from home.

When you suck it up and hit the road, your world view grows—and with it, your consciousness.

Try it. Just show up.

GENERATE SERENDIPITY

THIS IS HOW SERENDIPITY WORKS: EITHER YOU hope it happens or you make it happen.

When great things seem to fall out of the sky, sometimes it's just pure luck. Even though successful people don't like to admit it, most of them were lucky in one way or another, although sometimes the luck they had is hard to recognize. Maybe their luck was just not having bad luck. Lack of bad luck is truly one of the great blessings in life.

Even with luck, though, great things usually come because you've structured your life to put yourself in the path of opportunities, and sooner or later one comes your way. When it does, you're smart enough to grab it. Then once you've got hold of it, you make the absolute most of it, and create even more opportunities.

If you do all of that just right, some people—especially those who make no effort to create serendipity—may ascribe a beloved but scorned quality to you: just plain lucky.

Some people are insulted by that: "Me lucky? Like hell I am—I made my luck, and I'm proud of it!"

Don't bother to be insulted, or to try to sort circumstance from striving. Just take what you've got and keep your serendipity rolling downhill like a snowball, getting bigger and bigger. And keep your fingers crossed too, because shit happens. While you're crossing your fingers, though, it's also smart to create some contingency plans. Luck happens too, and it's just as important to prepare for good things as for bad.

A couple of years ago I was at an event called the Digital Media Exposition Convention, or DMEXCO, in Cologne, Germany. It's one of those global events I love to attend because you meet a lot of "lucky" people at them, and "luck," as you may have guessed by now, has the tendency to be contagious.

One guy I met was Charlie Crowe, who was the founder of the insanely important Festival of Media Global that I mentioned in Cheat 37. When Charlie saw me speak at DMEXCO, he was impressed. In my speeches I give everything I've got—and it pays off. So he comes over to me and he's like, "You should participate in the Festival of Media." The Festival is held at various venues all around the world, and Charlie set me up at two of the biggest, in Singapore and in Rome.

As I mentioned in that cheat, I gave the keynote in Rome, and killed it. And as luck would have it, my performance there snowballed into bigger things, including more business for Kiip.

Part of the reason it led to more good things, though, is because I kept *looking* for more good things. I look at every event I go to as a possible springboard to more opportunity. I never do something thinking that it's an end in itself.

If you look at something as if it's going to be a one-off situation, it will be. People with a shortsighted approach think, "Well, I lined up the fucking thing, so I'm gonna go in there, do my shit, be mediocre, and bounce." Then nothing comes from it, of course, so they think, "I knew it was just bullshit."

The moment you decide to be mediocre, you lose every follow-up opportunity that can come from it.

No matter what kind of presentation I'm giving—even if it's a private session with some businesspeople, or a quickie interview on television—I'm thinking about something I can get out of it, and that something usually happens.

The person who approaches me may not have something I really want, but so what? Maybe later on they will, or maybe they'll mention me to somebody else. Just being approached is flattering, good for motivation, and a sign I did something right.

The key is to be patient. If you expect an immediate payoff from everything, pretty soon you'll be doing nothing.

When you do line up something big, you gotta double down and give everything you've got, plus everything you'll ever have, even if you have to pull it out of your ass. It's amazing how much impact you can make with nothing but adrenaline and a big smile.

The takeaway: Make it your mission in life to aim for absolute excellence in all situations, because you never know what can come out of it. That is the essence of creating the snowball effect.

First you've got to know what the big moment is. That means research, studying your universe for opportunities that no one else sees, with risks or work that no one else wants.

Then you've got to hustle for it. Nobody serves opportunity on a platter. You've got to email people, then follow up, call them, follow up, see them, follow up, and stay tenacious until the doors finally open.

After that, you've got to go wherever that opportunity is, whether it's halfway around the world, in the worst part of town, or in some Podunk place in the middle of nowhere. Those places are—for your purposes, at least—all the same. They are where serendipity happens.

Then you grab it by the throat and don't let go.

Before you know it, you'll be rolling downhill with the

amount of speed and mass that define major momentum, and everything will fall into place right before your eyes.

It's a sweet moment—so electrifying that you can't even know how good it is until you've experienced it. It's like you're in a movie, playing yourself in a role that you wrote.

The people who don't want to see you succeed will jump out of the way as your snowball rockets down the mountain. The people who want to share your success will jump on. Everyone will ask, "How'd he *do* that?"

Somebody will say, "He was lucky." Somebody else will say, "He worked his ass off."

They'll both be right—and good luck trying to separate the luck from the work. Once the ball gets rolling, you can't.

TAKE ADVANTAGE OF THE GOLDEN AGE OF IDEAS WHILE YOU STILL CAN

YOU'RE ONE OF THE LUCKIEST PEOPLE IN THE history of world commerce.

I am too—we all are—because we were born into this rare and amazing window of opportunity, in which an intangible phenomenon has occurred that in most eras would have been impossible.

Here's the phenomenon: Ideas now drive money, even more than money drives ideas.

Think about it: There have always been people with great ideas, and many of them made great fortunes, but the deck was always stacked against them. Those people and their ideas weren't driving the action; money was. More precisely, the people who had money were driving the action. The people with money were kings, warlords, robber barons, tycoons, royal families, or political hustlers, and they were all ruthless. They used money as a weapon.

Then one fine day the Internet was invented, and the playing field was leveled in a way that had never been thought possible.

The day of the common man dawned.

This window may close—maybe before you even notice that

it's closing—so this is no time to kick back and wait for better days. The advent of computer technology and the Internet have created a vast frontier of incredible economic opportunity, and for once the power resides more in the individual than in the megaliths of big government and big business.

The historical tendency is for big guys to squeeze out little guys. Today it's the little guys who reign supreme. This balance of power may shift again—maybe even before you realize it's happening—but it hasn't happened yet, so saddle up! Find an idea and ride it.

The clearest economic indicator that Big Money has taken at least a temporary backseat to Big Ideas is that in the current structure of technology, especially in the Silicon Valley, there seem to be more investors than there are people with good ideas.

What this means—and bear with me while I take you back to that boring Economics 101 class—is that investor dollars are now in low demand but large supply, while ideas are in low supply but high demand. This puts the power in the hands of the idea generators, rather than the now dime-a-dozen financiers.

Yes, it's hard to crack open a new idea—but it's something anyone can do. It mostly just takes a brain, some balls, and a computer. Seriously, good ideas can come from *anywhere*. There are even great business ideas coming from a group of inmates in San Quentin prison that I'm working with through "The Last Mile Program" (if you're curious, Google it—it's amazing, and one of my investors started it), and the inmates don't even have access to computers.

So how do you come up with a great idea? There are no real guidelines; most are just a matter of common sense. There are a few mini cheats that can help, though. First is to avoid what I call the "Chitty Chitty Bang Bang trap." You might remember the kids' movie in which they built a totally sick car that could fly. It's something every kid fantasizes about. So why not build a totally sick flying car?

Because nobody needs it. Too complicated. Too expensive. You could sell about twenty of them, but you'd never get the capital to build even one, because there's zero market demand for them. Keep it simple, Simon.

Another mini cheat is to excavate the graveyard of undeveloped ideas and see if you can find some life in a concept that seems to be dead. Sometimes a person will come up with a great idea, but when they try to build their prototype, they *think* they're building Chitty Chitty Bang Bang, and so they throw up their hands in defeat.

People get rich following up on those ideas. Sometimes all it takes is a little more work. Or a lot more work. The harder the work, though, the more it's going to scare off potential competition. So challenge yourself. Take a shot. Go to the graveyard of great ideas, dig one up, and see if you can be the Dr. Frankenstein who brings it to life.

Another cheat is to do something that's so simple that everybody in the world wants to slap themselves for not thinking of it first. Like Uber. Or Airbnb. Those ideas were not rocket science. Sometimes the best ideas are the most obvious ones.

The big idea of this cheat is simple: We're in the golden age of ideas, a time when any individual—rich or poor, young or old—can rise up, seize a life-changing opportunity, and live the life that other generations could only dream of.

Wouldn't you like to be one of them?

FOCUS ON WHAT WON'T CHANGE

BECAUSE TECHNOLOGY CHANGES SO FAST, WE all see change as a constant these days. And in truth, it is.

Some things don't change. Find them, and you can make a fortune.

Yet focusing *solely* on change is a trap that catches a lot of people. People today are obsessed with finding "the next big thing." But there aren't that many new big things.

One version of "the next big thing" is to take something that exists and update it. However, the competition to reinvent the wheel is fierce—and sometimes pointless. The wheel already works pretty well.

People who drop out of the new-new rat race and *focus on what won't change* have a huge advantage.

This is something I learned from observing Jeff Bezos. When he came up with the idea of Amazon at the advent of Net commerce, he was thinking along the same general lines as a lot of people: "Shit's going to change. Like crazy."

But Bezos looked beyond the New and asked himself: "What *isn't* going to change? Two things: (1) customers are going to continue to want the best possible bargain, and (2) they are going to continue to want it delivered as fast as possible." The corollary to this logic was, "The only way I can go wrong is if people (1) start wanting to pay as much as possible and (2) insist on slow delivery."

His brilliance is almost comical.

It's no wonder that Bezos doesn't worry too much about immediate profitability. He's the whale in a sea of constantly shifting forces, sitting securely on solid ground in an essentially unglamorous business while everybody else tries to stay afloat on the choppy waters of change, racing each other to the new new, and capsizing every time the wind shifts.

If you'd rather be like Bezos, sitting pretty on the beach with an umbrella drink in your hand, look for classic, constant needs; classic styles; classic destinations; classic modes of expression, transportation, and communication. Tap into existing patterns of behavior. Classic will still be there long after the new new is old.

But look for the old classic with new eyes. Don't see the trees; see the forest. Don't see now; see forever. Don't see countries; see the world.

Then start looking for how to make that world just a little bit better.

TIE YOURSELF TO A GREATER VISION

LET'S SAY YOU GO INTO A MEETING AND YOU'RE trying to sell something. What you've got is pretty cool, and you feel cocky because your thing is better than your competitors' thing, so you expect a warm welcome. Only instead of cheers and applause, you get a big yawn or a politely phrased "fuck you." What went wrong?

Most likely you didn't tie yourself to a grander vision.

If you want to get people excited, don't go in there just talking about your cool new product. Go in there with a universal problem, like traffic: "I know you guys hate traffic. So do I. I've got a solution." That ties your cool new product to a problem they have.

In other words, tie your idea to something you know they care about, and that they realize everybody will care about. If you've got a great vision, pretty soon it won't be just yours—it'll be everybody's.

Google's vision was connecting the world's information, which before they came around really was not well connected. There were search engines, but they were nothing like Google's, and didn't excite passion and loyalty among the company's employees, customers, the media, or anyone else.

Google changed all that. Their warp-speed functionality and efficiency was so sick that it was like a noble cause. News flash: Not all noble causes need to be about world peace or hunger. If you can eliminate traffic jams or make the Internet work the way it should, you have something that's as powerful as almost any mission. Helping the average person by making his or her life just a little bit easier every day is a big deal, and worthy of being considered visionary.

A vision like Google's is so exciting that it leads to other grand visions. Google Earth and the Google Self-Driving Car Project are two examples. They inspire passion not just because they are cool, flashy products, but because they are part of a grander vision to make people's lives better through connectedness and information. These are the kinds of things that people don't just want to buy but want to be part of. Nobody wants to be part of something mediocre.

Disney is another company that tied itself to a concept: wholesome family values. The company practically invented the concept of high-quality family entertainment, long before it branched into films aimed at an older market and became a powerhouse studio and network. Now, even when it offers a product that is neither family-oriented nor high-quality, people forgive it, and wait for the next Disney blockbuster.

At Kiip, I make sure that everything we do and say aligns with our vision. I didn't go into meetings telling people that Kiip could create good ads. I went in there saying, "I know you guys hate to tap on banner ads. So do I. I've got a solution." I wasn't just offering a new form of interaction and engagement. I was offering a new way to help people fall in love with products. By rewarding the consumer during peak moments of achievement in apps and games with rewards, Kiip was building the kind of bond between products and consumers that ads just can't create.

I started with a big, true idea, and it caught on like wildfire.

That vision attracted some amazing people to our company. These people felt like they were creating the future, not just creating ads. Our work reflects this, and we wanted everyone in the industry to understand the "why" behind the model we were creating.

Our next step was to use the reputation of excellence we created to expand that vision. Although the idea started with simply rewarding users in games, that was too limiting—the market was finite. Then we realized a new truism: Users were experiencing achievement moments in all the apps they used every day, not just games. We tied our company to that vision, and started working with a variety of other mobile apps and sites.

That's when it got super-exciting.

And we're only a few years old, with many visions yet to appear. Everyone has a vision. What's yours?

MAKE RE-CREATION RECREATION

CREATIVITY IS ARGUABLY THE GREATEST OF ALL superpowers.

By definition, it's the heart and soul of start-ups because those companies—spoiler alert—start something. A start-up's core concept is almost always something created from nothing but the creativity of its founder.

Creativity is a necessary ingredient for any successful start-up. Opening a new car wash with your buddies is not really a start-up. That's been done. A start-up is opening a car wash that cleans cars in some new and unique way—something so much better than the old kind of car wash that people everywhere will want to do it that way.

That said, you don't need to pull ideas out of thin air to be creative. Creating something is generally a matter of re-creating something, even if the reinvention is as dramatic as the difference between an encyclopedia and the Internet.

You can tell the most ridiculously imaginative people in the world to come up with an idea of what an alien looks like, and almost all of the aliens will look essentially humanoid—arms, legs, head, eyes. That's because the only thing we've ever understood about a living being is that it's a component of appendages: a body and a head. It's almost impossible to imagine an intelligent being that doesn't follow those rules—even if you're one of the most imaginative people in the world.

The point is: If even our wildest imaginations are re-creations of existing things, so is everything else.

Creation doesn't even need to be an otherworldly vision. The creative genius of the Model T was that it was essentially a re-creation—albeit a revolutionary one—of the horse and buggy. Henry Ford didn't dream it up out of nowhere; he simply reinvented something that had been around for centuries in a way that no one had ever thought of, and it morphed from a dream into a reality that shot around the world.

TOSS YOUR CAP IN THE AIR

"AS I LOOK OUT UPON THIS SEA OF EAGER young faces . . ."

That's how a lot of people start school commencement speeches—so of course I don't.

I prefer "Helloooo!" with a fast hop to the podium and a big smile that says there's no place in the world that's more exciting than right here, right now.

That's how I started my most recent commencement address, in my hometown of Vancouver, B.C., at the very unique Bodwell High School, a private boarding school for hand-picked students. About 80 percent of them are international—from Russia, Asia, Latin America, and various places with rapidly growing economies—who come from cultures in which parents value education enough to let their kids go far from home for an amazing opportunity, no matter how much they'll miss them.

The title of my speech was "Being Young and Rocking It!" I knew the kids would like that, and my secondary agenda was to audition the central theme of *The Cheat Code*. I wanted to put it right in people's faces and see if they lit up. They did.

I'm sure that a lot of you readers of *The Cheat Code* are

young, or at least feel that way. When you're trying to put your own stamp on the world, it's easy to *feel* young: excited, hopeful, scared to start, and even more scared not to.

So here's the graduation speech version of *The Cheat Code*, rendered as seven talking points. Think of them as your Lucky Seven:

1. *Be yourself.* I started my speech with a great quote: "Be yourself, because everybody else is already taken." I reminded the kids that no matter how old they got, other people would always be trying to tell them who they really are and what they should be doing. But at the end of the day, I said, whatever these things are and whatever you do have to feel right to you. If you can answer yes to the question "Am I happy?" then whatever you're doing is right. If someone tells you otherwise, screw 'em.

2. *Reinvent and repurpose your weaknesses into strengths.* I knew these students had probably come to Canada thinking that they'd be at a big disadvantage going to school in a foreign country, learning in a non-native language. But almost without exception, they'd discovered that speaking another language fluently was a huge plus. This same experience, I said, would repeat itself forever. It's like a Jedi mind trick. You can easily transform what is typically perceived to be a weakness into a big strength. It's all in how you think about it.

3. *Audacity differentiates.* I told them to forget about fitting in, and find the best ways to be different. I urged them to hold with all their heart to the skills they'd learned from extracurricular activities back home, activities that weren't necessarily popular in Canada, because those would be skills that many Canadian kids didn't necessarily have. A fact that is both frightening and fantastic is that we all came off the same basic conveyor belt, but if you're the guy who knows how to build your own model, you've got something unique. Every special skill you've got will

someday become meaningful, and it'll happen when you least expect it. Those are the things that will ultimately make you stand out from everyone sitting next to you who graduated with the same degree. The more differentiated you are, the more indispensable you can become.

4. *Think big.* There's always a way to tweak an idea and make it absolutely massive. Don't think "I'm gonna build a plane." Think "I'm gonna build a rocket ship." (Or not. Elon Musk did that already. How about "I'm gonna build a jetpack"? No, NASA cornered that one. What about a whole new way to get to the moon! *Now* we're getting closer! Kiip thinking.)

5. *Just ask.* I love this mini cheat. So underrated. Always ask for something better than what's offered. If people say no, so what? If they say yes, awesome! No one knows how to help you if you don't know how to ask. What do you get if you don't ask for anything? That's easy: exactly what you asked for.

6. *Little things matter.* They didn't really want to hear it, but I told the students that the tiny things their parents forced them to do would soon pay off. You remember: Smile. Brush your teeth. Pick up after yourself. Plan ahead. Finish what you start. These are the seeming trivialities that sculpt the adults we become. As time passes and our power and responsibilities expand, so do these good habits, until one day finishing what you start turns into making one more little tweak on a tough project, and voilà—you've suddenly got a million-dollar discovery. It may seem like pointless nagging when you're a kid, but later on it all starts to make sense.

7. *Everything that exists was built by somebody.* Credit for the last one goes to Steve Jobs, who made a forty-second video out of the idea. It went so viral that half the people in tech needed antiretroviral therapy. Jobs was walking down the street one day when it hit him that no matter what he looked at—the traffic

lights, the sidewalks, the stores—everything had been created by a human being who was no smarter than him and millions of others. He saw with crystalline clarity that every person has the power and the potential to be a person who built something. When you realize that, you'll never be the same. When you build something, the world will never be the same.

That's it. Toss your cap into the air. But don't wait for it to fall.

Get busy.

The world is waiting.

MAKE LIKE A BLINDFOLDED RACE CAR DRIVER

COULD HAVE CALLED THIS CHEAT "THE ENTRE-preneur Mind Trick." You'll see why.

Entrepreneurship, as I've said elsewhere, can't be spoon-fed to you in school, so there must be another path to it, right?

There is, but it's not necessarily something you can see.

Here's an analogy: Last year I fulfilled one of my fantasies by learning to drive race cars. And shortly thereafter it dawned on me that being an entrepreneur is a bit like a race car driver . . . driving blindfolded.

Let me explain what I mean. First they put us through safety training, and showed us slides that revealed the proper techniques. Everybody walked out of class thinking they knew what they needed to know.

Then we went out on the course—an actual, professional track—and all that learning flew right out the window.

The point is, you can't teach car racing with slides. The value of the slides was in showing you that certain things would happen that would scare the shit out of you, but that you'd live . . . probably. The slides weren't really instruction—they were just psychotherapy.

The real learning came only when I raced the full track like a bat out of hell, over and over clocking hundreds of miles a day, to the point where I almost didn't even need to look at the road. It came when I got to the point where I knew every inch of the track and could feel it in my mind and body. When I knew, even without looking: when I'd hit the straightaways, where I'd need to mash down on the accelerator, when I'd arrived at the stretches where I should back off, turns where I needed to feather the brakes, and turns where I'd slam down on them. Same places, every time.

Professional drivers run the same tracks thousands of times. They can do it blindfolded. Literally. Well, probably literally. Nobody tries it, because that would be stupid. Fun—like in *Talladega Nights: The Ballad of Ricky Bobby*—but still stupid.

Navigating a racetrack purely by feel, in the same way a pianist navigates a keyboard without looking (and just like the muscle memory that governs all other sports), has a lot in common with entrepreneurship. You can learn muscle memory, but you can't teach it. You've got to let go, and let your brain and your body work it out on their own.

Entrepreneurship isn't something in which you consciously say: "I'm going to be an entrepreneur today! And the first step is this, then that. . . ." It's just a way you operate. A way you live your life. A style. An ethic. Like driving a race car, it turns you on.

That's why I resist people picking my brain on how to be an entrepreneur. They're really just asking for the equivalent of those training videos: glorified therapy sessions, so they won't be so scared.

You won't make it as an entrepreneur if you're not scared. Fear is your friend. If you're not scared, it means you're where somebody else has already been. Immediate disqualification. Go somewhere new.

When you're there, don't look for road signs. Just accept that you were born to be there.

At that point, you can call yourself an entrepreneur.

BUILD THE CHARACTER OF AN ENTREPRENEUR

THERE ARE CHARACTER TRAITS THAT ARE SO common among successful entrepreneurs that it seems as if these people had them in their DNA on the day they were born. They didn't.

In entrepreneurship, everything is earned and learned. But that doesn't mean that just anybody can earn and learn the character of an entrepreneur.

It gets even more complicated, and more exclusive, the closer you look.

Almost nobody develops these qualities and character from actually *being* an entrepreneur. Generally, you become an entrepreneur because you earned and learned them somewhere else. And if you don't have most of them by now, your road to entrepreneurship may be rocky.

If you've got them, though, you're already well on your way, and just need to find the right project, right people, right time, and right place to put them to work. So what are these elusive qualities that make a great entrepreneur?

Start with trust. You've got to be able to grant an almost blind trust in the special people in your life. If you can't give that to your business team, they won't have the room and the confidence they need to create excellence.

You can't hand out trust like candy, though, or you'll get burned beyond recognition. Part of the learned aspect of this quality is being able to sort out the people who will help you from the people who will fuck you. If you keep the ratio in your favor, you'll do fine.

You also need intensely thick skin. If you're successful, you will be insulted, doubted, and double-crossed; in fact, the more successful you become, the more often this will happen. Don't take it personally. Don't dwell on it. Sometimes it's just a tactic, sometimes it's just bullshit, and sometimes it's something you can learn from. Pull anything positive from it that you can, and move on.

Learn to compartmentalize. If your boyfriend dumps you, somebody steals your credit cards, and your best friend is the reason your boyfriend dumped you, show up for work like it never happened. It has nothing to do with work. Ignore it. Walk it off. If your first meeting of the day is a disaster, go into the next one like it never happened. There's a time and place to sort out your emotions and grow from your losses. Real time is not that time. Real time is each discrete moment, in and of itself, each born anew. Revel in the fact that real time is separate from all the other bullshit.

Be pit-bull tenacious and relentless. These may sound like they're the exact same thing, but they're actually somewhat different: Tenacity is the ability to endure bad things, and relentlessness is the drive to pursue good things. They're a good team. With either quality, you've got to have the conviction, even on the darkest days, that you can succeed. Tenacity and relentlessness will energize you to the point where you become almost impervious to fatigue. They offer you a constant state of excitement.

There's one little drawback: You only learn tenacity from getting beaten down. If you've always had things handed to you on a platter, it's not a quality that will come naturally to you. I don't see a lot of great entrepreneurs who were born with a silver spoon in their mouth. But I do see some, because having advantages can be great for developing relentlessness. People who come from success expect success, and so they are more likely to relentlessly go after it. Those who allow that privilege to make them lazy never get anywhere, of course. But those who are happy to work their asses off do well, especially if they're lucky enough to avoid huge, demoralizing setbacks—or develop the tenacity to endure them. The tiny minority of people who combine privilege, tenacity, and relentlessness are absolutely deadly.

Resourcefulness is another must. You need to know exactly what resources are at your disposal, and how you can rearrange the pieces on your proverbial chessboard to use each and every one to your maximum advantage. If you've got very limited resources, you've got to learn to make something out of nothing. That's hard—but great entrepreneurs do it all the time. One way they do it is to bluff. If you're good at bluffing, you can leap over obstacles like they're not even there. One caveat: When you do bluff, you'd better have a good fallback position. Reckless bluffing is so transparent that not even you will believe your bullshit, and people will smell your fear and kick your ass out the door.

Bluffing's bigger, better brother is confidence, another indispensable quality. You need to believe—really believe, and not just kid yourself—that you've got something great. Your belief will make that thing real. You've got to be so good at convincing yourself that your belief in yourself becomes contagious. When you're with someone who is truly confident, you cannot distinguish whether what they've got is real or if they're just pulling it out of their ass—and you don't care! I know, it's really insane.

But the best entrepreneurs are insane, in the positive sense of the word.

Empathy really matters. Not sympathy, though, because even though that's a valid, kind emotion, it's one that's says: "Yeah, you're fucked." That's just not productive. Empathy simply says: "I know how you feel." It doesn't convey hopelessness.

Empathy also includes the ability to put yourself in somebody else's shoes when there is no particular problem. In that way, it's a lot like intuition. An empathetic, intuitive person can size someone up in thirty seconds and know exactly how to sway them.

The active aspect of empathetic intuition is persuasion. Think about those people who are so good at making you do things that you think it was your own idea. In those situations, the person simply recognized what you wanted and gave you a good reason to pursue it. That's the power of persuasion. Another element of persuasion is observational skill, sometimes referred to as sensitivity. If you're sensitive, you don't always need to put yourself in somebody else's shoes to see how they feel, and you don't need to rely on the intangible element of intuition. You just watch people. You study their body language, their tone, the way they relate to others, how they dress, who they know, and what they like. You play Sherlock Holmes. It's not rocket science. All of these qualities are sometimes rolled together into what people now call emotional intelligence. Here's the ultimate cheat on having high emotional intelligence: Be the best you. Be what your parents tried to teach you to be when you were a kid: a good, confident, ambitious, strong person, who sincerely cares about others and really pays attention to them. I know, it was hard to do then, and it's hard now. Start by taking an honest look at yourself. See if you're close to being the best possible you. If you are, you've learned the character that makes a great entrepreneur.

TAKE MOON SHOTS

MY FAVORITE ENTREPRENEURS ARE THE ONES who literally don't care what other people think.

Those are the people who have built their own model for success and execute like machines. They don't care about people's perceptions or opinions, or anything at all, for that matter, except their vision. They're almost blindly obsessed with what they're creating, and they don't do it for the glory of people complimenting them.

They do it because they have this burning itch. They feel like they *have* to create something new. They think that if they don't, it's going to almost dismantle them. Their goals are practically an obsession. In a way, they're obsessed with being obsessed.

I admire the people who are obsessed, because only truly obsessed people are likely to go as far as they need to in order to execute their ideas, and do it all successfully. It's like somebody has cast a spell over them—or they've cast it over themselves—and they're in a kind of trance. Some of them won't snap out of it until they actually get it done. Occasionally they'll put so much into it that they almost die trying.

One way to know if you have this quality is if you feel like you just can't be half in or half out. The people who feel like they can still do something by being only half in will probably be half successful. These are usually people who build their business around their lifestyle, instead of building their life around their business. They're doing it to make a living—to build an income stream that helps them maintain their current standard of living without interfering with the other things they love to do. Some people are okay with that, and plenty of them make a perfectly sustainable income that feeds their family and allows them to have a great life.

If that's what you want, fine. But I'd personally rather be one of those balls-to-the-wall moon shot entrepreneurs who aren't trying to preserve anything and who just love what they're doing. For them, entrepreneurship *is* their lifestyle, and sometimes they don't even give a shit about making money from it. They just do it because it's what they love.

For some of these people, it's almost like they intentionally pick things that look impossible, just because that's what it takes to really have an impact on the world. It's that impact that gives them a gleam in their eye. Or sometimes it's just the sheer impossibility of it—the fear factor—that ignites that electrifying spark.

There's another, even crazier type of entrepreneur who seems to have the opportunity to make all the money they want, but they spend every penny obsessing over their passion. Those are the ones that are insanely messed up in the head—but are awesome. You cannot know what they will do. Maybe their idea will result in an astonishing, world-changing, mind-altering outcome—or maybe it will just turn out to be a fabulous funeral pyre. These are the people who know how to accept both outcomes. They've seen the worst that could happen and aren't fazed by it at all.

I love to meet those people. It's just so cool to relate to them when you're trying to figure out what problem they're so obsessed with. They're so passionate, so excitable, that it's just refreshing.

These are the people who are almost literally shooting for the moon, and it's almost impossible not to feel inspired by them.

DISPLAY THE INTELLECT OF AN ENTREPRENEUR

THE GOOD NEWS IS THAT YOU DON'T NEED TO be insanely smart to be insanely successful.

The better news is that there's never a day when you can put your brain on autopilot and coast. As an entrepreneur, you're creating your life and your company moment by moment, and each moment counts.

If the second part—the better news—sounded like bad news, you're probably not a natural entrepreneur.

There are tens of millions of people who love to chill at work and go through the motions of fulfilling a reasonable minimum of their duties. It's less taxing, no doubt about it, and there's nothing wrong with wanting to avoid stress.

However, that's not the intellectual mind-set of entrepreneurship. Entrepreneurs would rather be excited than relaxed. They'd rather be challenged than comfortable. Instead of avoiding stress, they relish it because it adds to their sense of accomplishment.

It's good for an entrepreneur to have a high IQ because that helps with learning and retention. Even so, graduating at the top of your class or being a MENSA member is not a requirement for entrepreneurial achievement. This sort of intellectual status is probably a greater asset in the conventional corporate world, but even the biggest companies don't place artificial requirements on anyone's IQ anymore.

The most fundamental, indispensable intellectual quality of a successful entrepreneur, in my opinion, is that they are simultaneously logical and creative. They see the obvious, which sounds easy but isn't. They can sort things out. They can understand and explain complicated things to ordinary people. They can break down complex problems without getting tangled up in details that don't matter and without missing details that do matter.

Successful entrepreneurs are constantly ingesting information and then relaying it to the right people as efficiently as possible. They make sure that everybody understands the basic issues and that everyone is working together to achieve the same, shared goal.

This kind of problem management is not brain surgery. That's why you don't need to be Einstein. Ironically, though, an actual brain surgeon—whose gifts lie in the minutiae and who generally have no special affinity for team projects—might find entrepreneurship more difficult than brain surgery.

So don't worry about being brilliant. Worry about coming up with brilliant ideas.

FUCK LUCK

LUCK, LIKE SHIT, HAPPENS. YOU DON'T HAVE much to say about it.

As I mentioned in Cheat 53, lots of people think serendipity is the same thing as luck, but it isn't. Serendipity—defined as a valuable, unexpected occurrence—doesn't just happen. Serendipity is luck that happens when you keep your eyes open.

Probably the most serendipitous thing that ever happened to me was when I was playing hockey at age 15. At that age, I didn't match up to most of the other guys in muscle power, but I played balls-to-the-wall and held up well, which was great for my self-esteem—until the day my knee got hit so hard that it almost shattered the lower growth plate in my femur. That would have stunted the growth in my leg forever, but it missed the plate by a millimeter. That was *lucky*!

The doctor at the ER initially took an X-ray and saw nothing, so he told me I had a tendon tear and that I should go home and try to limit my walking until it mended. If I had, I would have walked with a limp for the rest of my life. My mother is a nurse, though, and she didn't agree, and was able to bump me to first in line for an MRI, which revealed the fracture. That was serendipitous! Not just because it kept my leg intact, but because when your mother does something like that for you, it creates gratitude and respect that you remember all your life.

For about a year after the injury, I was in a wheelchair and on crutches, and had to depend on my mom and dad and friends to do the most basic things for me. Here are the likely pastimes for a teenage boy who is suddenly disabled: playing video games, watching a lot of porn, or developing an intimate relationship with Marvel Comics. I chose a different option. I decided to sharpen my design skills using online tutorials, which proved to be a huge stroke of serendipity, because that's what kick-started my career. If you're thinking, "That was a matter of choice, not serendipity," you're giving me too much credit. The other three natural proclivities get old in a big hurry, even for a teenage male. In any case, I discovered that my mind was as hungry for exercise as my busted leg was.

The greater serendipity during my rehab, though, was finding out how truly generous my family and friends were. That's something you can't fully comprehend until life knocks you down. But I squeezed an even greater serendipity out of it:

I discovered that even a teenage kid can start a company.

Two days before I wrote this, I got back on the ice for the first time since my injury—and I was as nervous as a ten-year-old, despite now being the CEO of an international company. I'd already practiced a few times, but I was super-rusty, was pretty sure that I didn't have the stamina to play a full game, and knew it was going to hurt my pride when I had to punk out.

Then one of the guys on our team got in a fight and was kicked out of the game. Shit! There was nobody to sub in, and I was already spent. Bad luck!

But fuck luck—it was serendipity! I sucked it up, played way better than I could have done by choice, and pushed myself so hard that I was too exhausted to even drive myself home.

But I did get home, slept like a baby, and woke up with that rare sense of physical confidence that you can acquire only by pushing your body beyond what's normally possible. You can't get that kind of rush from making money, or traveling the world, or being on the cover of a magazine.

It touched some emotions I hadn't felt in ages—nine years, to be exact. And now I can't wait to get back on the ice.

Fuck luck. Serendipity happens, and it feels amazing.

WRITE IT DOWN

A GOOD ACTOR—AND REMEMBER THAT ALL EN-trepreneurs are good actors—can make a story come to life right before your eyes. A great actor can do that with mostly just body language.

I've seen hundreds of sales meetings where the salesperson puts on such a memorable performance that somebody should have been filming it. Their ideas come alive, and captivate the hearts of the audience much like a Broadway star might.

But that doesn't make the ideas good. The concept can be dumb as dog shit and still seem like a good idea at the time.

Reality makes its welcome appearance, though, the moment you start putting things on paper. When you do that, you can usually tell in one or two pages if an idea is smart or stupid. The smaller the words, the better. No analogies, no allegories, no stories. Just plain facts.

Everything before the written word is just more clutter in the ether. It's nothing but somebody talking into thin air.

Amazon knows this. Before I made my first pitch to Amazon's partnership teams, they told me that they would prefer I not use PowerPoint. They don't want somebody to draw them a picture or put on a performance. They're all about the written word, fully formed—explaining in layman's terms exactly what the proposal or project is, preferably in one paragraph. It makes sense to force yourself into a format that kiips everything in perspective. Writing it down is one way to do this, and it works.

Writing things down also provides another huge advantage: You remember them. It kills me to be saying something so obvious, but I'm afraid it's not obvious to a lot of people.

I've been in tons of meetings where I look around, and it's like: "Who is taking notes? Anybody? Just me?"

When I'm in one of those meetings and it's with people who work with me, I say, "Why are you not writing this down?" And they say: "Oh, I'll remember it." Which is when I say, "No, you won't!"

And then I feel like a parent, but I can't afford to just blow it off. I need them to remember.

There were too many times when somebody said, "What was it you told me to do on that project?" Then I have to look it up— because I *do* write stuff down—and tell them again. If there's one thing I don't like, it's having to tell somebody the same thing twice.

It's not just a matter of doubling my workload. It makes me wonder: "What else did they forget? I hope it's not something that's going to hurt the company."

Another advantage of note-taking is that it triples your brain's access to the memory. Note-taking adds a kinesthetic and visual memory to the auditory one.

It goes even further. If you don't write things down, you end up cluttering your mind, leaving less memory storage for more important things and less brain capacity for other processes, including creativity.

When you relieve your brain of unnecessary burdens, you

leave more space open for momentous ideas. If you're really smart, you develop dirt-simple systems that even let you free your mind from having to remember trivialities such as where you left your car keys—like always leaving them in the same place.

Eleanor Roosevelt—the most powerful person ever to live in the White House without being president—is reported to have once said, "Small minds talk about people, average minds talk about events, and great minds talk about ideas." Here's a logical extension: Teeny-tiny minds talk about where their car keys are.

The digital era makes it easier than ever to record memories. After all, the absolute essence of the computer is memory, and when this function is used optimally, it advances human thought exponentially. We can effectively use computers to consciously erase trivialities from our brains' frontal lobes.

We're already seeing that digital power transform some of the most mentally advanced professions, including those of doctors and lawyers. Before computerization, physicians and attorneys needed to have such an incredible memory for details that it curtailed their abilities in other areas. Now that computers make a vast database of medical and legal information immediately available at the click of a mouse, doctors and lawyers can focus on other things, such as being more creative, empathetic, and able to perceive a situation holistically.

On the most basic level, taking notes is just a sign of being organized. How long do poorly organized people last at Kiip? Not long, and that's all I need to remember. What's the average length of their employment? I have no idea, but if you give me a minute to look at my files, I can tell you. I certainly can't remember.

EMBRACE THE POWER OF TWO

OUR CULTURE'S MYTHOLOGY AROUND THE ideal of the rugged individual, combined with all the hyped-up media stories of the brilliant lone entrepreneur coming up with a billion-dollar idea while tinkering in his basement or building a computer in his garage, has led to the recent celebration of the often-referenced "power of one." But really, there's more power in two. Three is even better, and four is better yet.

The greatest power in the power of one is getting those other people on board. There is no significant company that consists of just one person; the path to greatness simply can't be traveled alone.

Some people measure their success by how much they can do without any help. But *real* success invariably includes the ability to bring people together and to create a whole that's bigger than the sum of its parts—a whole that's made more powerful by the strength of shared visions and goals.

If you're the founder of a start-up or are in the first wave of any entrepreneurial endeavor, your first important job is to find the right people to fight alongside you: people who will be like loyal brothers and sisters—people who are brilliant, genuinely kind, fun to work with, and tolerant of ambiguity.

You are essentially the team captain. It's your job to pick a winning team.

The main thing, particularly in the beginning, is to find people who can do what nobody else on the team can. If everyone has the exact same skills and strengths, you're digging yourself into a hole of wasted money and probably dissension.

The best teams are built thoughtfully, to ensure that everyone's goals, values, and ideals are aligned. When this happens, great things just start coming together naturally. Success feels effortless, like it was inevitable.

People often use the analogy of the team captain when they talk about leadership. But in reality, if you're a manager or a team leader, you're less like the team captain and more like a train conductor.

Why? When you're the conductor, you're usually the only one who knows what the final destination is—or even the day-to-day direction. It's not always valuable for the whole team to know, because you need to have some people who are totally focused on excellence in their own piece of the puzzle. If everybody tries to have the big picture, it can get in the way, especially when you need to change course.

As the conductor, you need to have a certain degree of distance from the team to do your job. Sometimes you almost have to remove yourself physically, and other times mentally, as if you're having an out-of-body experience. It's easier to fix systematic problems when you see them from a bit of a distance rather than close up.

Despite the need for the conductor to stay focused on the big picture and coalesce each element of the team into a whole, there's also a fractal element to companies—meaning that often, each small piece mirrors the whole, in a different scale. So you need to understand all the working parts and be able to dive in at any given moment and help somebody who's struggling with something specific.

That's part of the reason it's good to know the company from top to bottom, and have a little experience in almost every type of job. In start-ups, that usually comes naturally, because in the beginning you need to do a little of everything. It's even more valuable just to be open and intuitive, and capable of turning on your creative juices at any time.

Even if you're the best team builder in the world, though, you'll probably never be a CEO if you don't have at least one superpower. Managers, of course, can come in at any stage of a company and build effective teams, but managers aren't owners.

Great entrepreneurs—the founders and CEOs—know exactly what their superpowers are (see Cheat 16), and they use them almost every day. The superpower can be almost anything—mastery of business skills, technology, public speaking, sales, or whatever—but it needs to be an important function that nobody in the company does better. The founder or creator will always be the foundation that a team is built on, and that foundation is irreplaceable.

Nothing is a sadder sight, though, than a piece of land with just a foundation on it and no building. You might be the one who builds the team, but it's the team who builds the majestic skyscraper.

GO!

A LOT OF PEOPLE MESS UP BY LIMITING ALMOST all their business to the phone, email, Skype, text, or videoconference. This misses the big point. It keeps you in your comfort zone, limits the expression of your full personality, and lets you hide your lack of preparation behind notes, scripts, and digital props. Actually going to a meeting makes you stand out. People see your face, smile, handshake, eye contact, charm, spontaneity, wit, and ability to think on your feet. They're flattered that you came, and maybe you end up socializing. You become a human being, rather than just a business entity. You might even become a friend.

As international olive oil importer Michael Corleone once said, "It's never just business. It's always personal."

Here's a problem: You've got to get there. That usually means traveling. Flying is hard. If you could just snap your fingers and be there, you'd do it almost every time.

Here's how to make it easier. That's important. Easy is good. Hard is bad.

Pack light. For almost all domestic trips, just take a carry-on. When you use a carry-on, you don't wait at the carousel, freaking out while your luggage fails to appear—especially when it's a business trip, since you've got documents, devices, and even clothes you can't replace. Sub-cheat: Even if you do check your luggage, carry all the indispensables.

Book your flights on a Wednesday, when airlines almost always sell them cheaper. If other people book your travel, make sure they know that money matters. Three of the main myths about money are (1) that people who have money don't *worry* as much about it as people who don't have it; (2) that people who have money don't *work* as hard as people who don't have it; and (3) that people who have money don't try as hard to *keep it* as people who don't have it. If your assistants believe any of those myths, they shouldn't be spending your money.

Get an aisle seat as close to the front as possible. You'll be one of the first people off—and you can use the restroom without stepping over people, which is a big deal on a long flight, especially if people in your row are asleep.

Don't show up too early to the airport. If you're late, you can legitimately assert your need for priority in the security line. Join every airline membership program you can, so you can begin to accumulate miles. Before you know it, you'll be in at least a couple of programs that will let you go into the expedited lanes. Some people go through those lanes no matter what, because it's typically considered bad customer service to insist on seeing the membership card that would entitle you to use them. If you ask for boarding gate priority, it's also easier to do it in those shorter lanes—fewer bad vibes. Airport lines reward late people (if you ask the right way). In some ways, they also punish early people—so arriving later makes sense.

To sleep, don't screw around with the pillows and blankets, because those don't help. Fly late in the day, or at night, when you're tired. If necessary, drink a glass of wine, or take a pharmaceutical relaxant, if you don't have to drive when you get there. Don't waste your time reading magazines or playing with devices. Put something in your Kindle or tablet you need to read, but try not to work on things that require full focus.

Book a hotel that's as convenient and quiet as absolutely possible, and don't worry about frivolous amenities. The important amenity is room service, which can be a lifesaver if you have an early-morning meeting or want to work while you eat.

Exercise counts, because your body counts. But try to get it by walking around the city and absorbing the ambiance, instead of in a forgettable fitness room. Seeing a new place is an education in itself, especially if you're abroad. It also gives you some commonality with whomever you're there to see.

If you want to create some indelible memories of a new place, listen to a very small playlist with new songs while you walk around. Later, every time you hear those songs they'll bring back the city's sights, sounds, smells, and ambiance.

There is no such thing as a boring city—just boring travelers. People live there for a reason. Find out the easy way: Ask somebody. Just asking people about their city is an education.

The easier your travels, the wider they will be, and with them, your view of the world.

The more you see the many different worlds that people live in, the more you'll love the earth, and feel right at home anywhere.

BE MONEY

RAISING INVESTMENT CAPITAL IS EASIER NOW than it's ever been. The whole landscape has changed.

True, the age-old investor criteria—dominated basically by risk and reward—still stand. But the tools, terms, and mechanisms of investment are always in flux as business environments morph.

Recently there have been massive changes in the investor landscape, much of it ushered in by a 2012 law: the Jumpstart Our Business Startups Act, also known as the JOBS Act. It eliminated a lot of red tape and allowed many more people to invest, with greater flexibility. Investors can now put their money into a company without having to get accredited by the government, and they can offer to buy any increment of a company that they want.

This opened the door to dramatically new types of investment sources, like Kickstarter, the global crowdfunding platform. It seemed to come out of nowhere, and yet facilitated the investment of about $1.5 billion in its first six years, from almost eight million different backers. At first it seemed as if Kickstarter might be just a frivolous toy for hobbyists and dilettantes, because in the beginning so many of the projects were marginal or unrealistic, but it exploded—mostly because of the incredible reach of the Internet—and today has funded some game-changing products and ideas.

The goal of Kickstarter is simple: to give entrepreneurs and inventors who may have been turned down by traditional funding sources the opportunity to kick-start their projects by amassing small contributions from a large number of people. If ten thousand people each invest $10 in something, the total investment comes to $1 million, enough to generously finance the vast majority of start-ups. And, thanks to Kickstarter, it turns out to be a hell of a lot easier to raise $10 ten thousand times than $1 million just once.

Pebble Smartwatch is an example of a company that was having trouble raising money from the traditional sources, so they launched a Kickstarter campaign in 2012, with the goal of $100,000. Backers who put in $115 were promised a watch if and when the company reached their target number. They made the goal in just two hours, and then went on to raise close to $5 million more the first week. They rolled out their second-generation watch, Pebble Time, in 2015, and about seventy-eight thousand backers pledged over $20 million.

Things were very different when I raised my first dollar in 2010, during the Great Recession. At that time, the options I had in front of me were very limited compared to now. Serious investors were confined to mostly two types: the angel investor, a rich person who invests in start-ups in exchange for partial ownership, and the venture capitalist, who works for a fund that pools the resources of large numbers of people, firms, and other funds.

These days, when somebody asks me for advice about securing a first-round investment, my answer is: "You are in luck, my friend! There's now almost a glut of early, seed-stage investors."

Because there are so many new sources of capital, this is the best time ever to have an idea, and a friend to build it with.

There are now incubators that help start-ups with everything from access to investors to helping them find office space to management training. There's also a slightly different version of incubators, called accelerators, that get more involved with companies that are already operating but are still very young. The incubators and accelerators help establish a lot of start-ups, knowing that many will fail, because it only takes a few major successes for them to reap huge benefits.

Plus, these days, investing in start-ups is *cool*. The status symbol in Silicon Valley—akin to the New York symbol of having a house in the Hamptons, or the L.A. symbol of driving a Rolls—is how many companies you've invested in.

As I mentioned in Cheat 54, there is also an extremely high ratio of investors to start-ups in the Valley right now. People say—and it's not entirely a joke—that there's more money than start-ups to spend it on.

The success of the first huge wave of entrepreneurs has made it easier for the succeeding waves. It no longer seems like such a shot in the dark.

The sheer numbers of people involved in the new start-up subculture—along with the ease of communication among them—also makes it easier to find money. Everybody seems to know everybody, and a great many investments come from personal relationships—not out of friendship, because even friends don't throw their money at bad ideas, but out of connectivity. For instance, the initial investors in Uber were just a small club of people who were really good friends.

After about five years of running Kiip, I've had around thirty investors, and not one of them came out of nowhere. We always had a mutual connection.

Even so, as always happens when abundance diminishes scarcity, the value of connections is dropping. It's just too easy now, especially with the almost constant round of meet-up conventions, to say that you know somebody. It's like, "Yeah, I know Brian. Cool guy! I handed him some ice cream in Austin." A few years ago that would have meant something, but today it's just one of a million random connections.

Even without connections, though, there are ways to establish your credibility in your first round of investment. Investors are interested in the companies you've worked for, what you've achieved, whether you've previously started another company, why you aren't still there, whom you've worked with, and who is on your team now. There are other, even more abstract signals that you're a valid target for investment, like: "Are you tolerant of risk?" "What's your motivation for doing this?" "What's your five-year goal?" "What's your dream?" "Whom do you admire?" "What do you post on Instagram?"

They're looking at you as much as at your project. They know that your first ideas about your company will probably not be what you end up with, because as you scale out the company, the environment will change. As my investor John Callaghan says, "Ideas fail, but people don't."

If investors get any whiff of you being a shitty person, they won't touch you, even if you've got the greatest idea ever. They're looking for people who can lead teams that take ideas from start to finish. They want somebody who works with devotion, inspiration, confidence, and an insane amount of perseverance. Investors already have money; what they're looking for is passion.

So however you choose to pursue funding for your project—

whether through a crowdfunding site like Kickstarter, an incubator like Y-Combinator, or the more traditional route—don't go to potential funders thinking that you've got it made just because this is a golden age for finding investors. The same rules that once applied still apply. Money seeks money.

My best advice: Be money.

CHOOSE YOUR INVESTORS WISELY

I LOVE KIIP'S INVESTORS. BECAUSE THEY GAVE ME money? No. It's the other way around. I love them because they're great people—and that's why they gave me money.

Substantial investment money is hard to get, especially for a start-up. But what a lot of entrepreneurs don't realize is that funding can come from many sources, just as great entrepreneurial ideas can come from any number of places of inspiration. The key isn't just finding money; it's finding the right fit between the investor and the entrepreneur.

My investors are the perfect fit for me, and I try hard to be the perfect fit for them. When you find someone who's the perfect fit for you—whether in romance, friendship, or business—it's impossible not to like them and think they're great, because your mutual goals and interests align.

The feeling has to be real, though. You can't fake liking some investors just so they'll give you money. First of all, those people are way too smart to believe that you like them if you actually don't. They hear dozens of pitches a day and have bullshit detectors hardwired into their brains. They've heard it all, and will know—probably even before you do—if you're the right fit.

You've got to be on the same wavelength, emotionally and morally. You've got to have the same basic intellectual interests and abilities. You've got to share a similar vision and level of energy.

Sounds kind of like a marriage, doesn't it?

Like a marriage or a super-close friendship, not only can't you fake it, you also can't force it. The best advice you can give somebody who's looking to find Mr. or Ms. Perfect is never to settle. Don't think you can change somebody, don't go after somebody based on just one element, and don't try to change yourself to win their affection. The same is true of investors in a business.

I love my investors, and sometimes—especially early in the relationship—I talk to them even more than I talk to my mom or my best friends. That doesn't mean, though, that my investors *are* my best friends. We have a great relationship, but it's important to keep that relationship on a business level, because there are core things they need to do that could be complicated by too close a personal friendship with you. They have their own objectives and agendas, and at the end of the day they're there because they want a return on their investments—not to listen to your troubles or make you feel good.

What's the most important ingredient for a successful relationship between investor and entrepreneur? Transparency. That's why I bring my investors in on my business process, in the same way that I sometimes share my plans with my customers. I go over my six-month plans with them so that they can feel like they've become part of my brain and share my enthusiasm. There's nothing more bonding than bringing someone into your inner circle.

When an idea they helped me with hatches and turns out great, I can see the gleam in their eyes when we talk about it. It's not just a good feeling for everybody; it's also good for business.

But as important as transparency is, drawing boundaries comes in at a close second. I respect their advice tremendously, but I don't kid myself that they know my business as well as I do. It would be scary for us if they did. I'm the one working in the trenches every day, so I don't have the unrealistic expectation that they'll be able to answer every pressing question that comes up. If I did think that, I'd be vulnerable to getting seriously sidetracked by the advice of somebody who hasn't had the time or information to think something through as carefully as I do.

Another thing that I love about my investors—people like Kevin Talbot, of Relay Ventures; Phil Black and Adam D'Augelli, of True Ventures; and Lars Leckie, of Hummer Winblad—is that they refused to take advantage of me at a time when they could have. They made that choice not just for my sake but for theirs as well. When I was in the traction round of gathering investors, after the first seed round, they easily could have messed with me by asking for a much larger stake for the same amount of investment dollars. And I probably would have taken their offer, because I was super-naive and on one level had no idea what I was doing. But they were smart enough, and decent enough, to know that if they did that, they'd be more than just investors. That it would be their company even more than mine, and that would create the possibility that I would lose some of my passion for it, or allow them to make decisions I should be making, as the guy with the boots on the ground. Then, if the company did succeed beyond our expectations, they'd need to be concerned that I would come back to them thinking that they hadn't taken care of me from the get-go.

Now that many of our dreams *have* been fulfilled, instead of being resentful, I'm more than grateful. I'm one of their biggest fans, and I vouch for them whenever they want to get into other deals. Who's a better advocate for an investor than somebody they've invested in?

The other savvy and considerate thing they did was *not* to go, "Yeah, I'll invest in you if you change this or that." Investors do that sometimes, and after the start-up goes out, retools, and comes back, the investor will go, "Well, I don't really feel like investing now—the timing's not right." They've just wasted your time and money by making you change your model and then not investing.

In other cheats I've talked about the importance of getting a great core group of supporters together and sticking with them, and your investors are definitely part of your core group. So when deciding which investors to "go to bed with," my advice is this: Choose people with whom you want to spend the next five years of your life—not just people good for a one-night stand. Choose the kind of investor you'll love, and who'll love you. Choose the people who know that "ideas fail—people don't."

This cheat works both ways. If you find the right people to invest in you, it will be somebody who's looking for the right people to invest in.

GO TO MUSEUMS

MUSEUMS ARE ONE OF THE GREAT CHEATS OF humankind. They're specifically designed to cut to the core of greatness, without revealing all the labor that led there. They're the equivalent of vitamins for the brain, with specific neurological nutrients distilled into their purest form.

They give you every imaginable way to stretch your brain. You end up seeing the world in a whole different way. You don't have to see every exhibit, or take the tour. Just wander and wonder. The museum will rub off on you, even if you don't intend it to.

If you allow it to be, the experience can mimic a virtual rebirth, re-creating those earliest moments of your infancy when your brain was flooded with so much sensory overload that it literally had to prune neuronal pathways to remain functional.

Go to museums to get a glimpse of what existed long ago, or far away, or in the mind of a person you'll never meet.

It's inspiring, if you allow it to be.

If you don't let it be, it's nothing—just a boring field trip for people who aren't ready to open up.

"Inspiration," of course, has another, physiological meaning: breathing in, or opening your lungs. So go to museums, stand in awe before a work of art, either visual or technological, and take a deep breath. Let in the art. Let out the breath. You'll be different.

I've been to hundreds of museums in about a hundred different countries. It's my favorite recreational activity.

I walk in with my eyes open, and I walk out with my mind open. With the best of luck, I walk out with my heart open as well.

GO BEYOND BINARY

I'M KNOWN AS SOMEBODY WHO'S HARD TO freak out. Every time some seemingly end-of-the-world crisis hits our company, or somebody in the company, or one of our close associates, and people start running around like their hair is on fire, I need to stay cool.

People assume it's because I've seen it all and been through everything. True, I have seen a lot of things, but not *everything*. I'm twenty-five—do the math.

I've been through everything in my mind, though. I'm always thinking through and imagining what plan B is, when to bail, and when to go balls-to-the-wall into war. That's what entrepreneurs do.

An entrepreneur doesn't have the luxury of corporate security, so staying cool in the face of insecurity is second nature to us. We don't look for security in what we have or in what our profits look like. Those are just the accoutrements of security. True security starts in the heart and stays there. It's much more mental than material.

Here's a sweet cheat for keeping that golden sense of security close to your heart: Learn to look for the Third Way.

Most problems seem on the surface to be solvable with binary solutions: invest or divest, dismiss or retain, spend or save. That orderly system of analysis is Western culture's classic method of rational thinking—*literally* classic, since it started with the Socratic method, when Socrates and his buddies sat under trees, untangling reason from mythology and emotion.

But it's no longer optimally functional. The modern era's bottomless cybercloud of information has rendered it obsolete, simply by revealing a whole new universe of options accessible with a single click. But the best entrepreneurs are creative enough to do the clicking in their own heads.

Finding the Third Way is the new classic method of problem solving.

The Third Way almost never jumps out at you on your first search (literal or figurative). It takes extra thinking, research, innovation, strategizing, game planning, and meta-gaming—but it's there, waiting for you to find it.

The Third Way is more than just the middle ground, or a compromise. Those were the early connotations of the term, when it originated in the 1950s, as a problem-solving device both in politics (primarily right-wing versus left-wing) and economics (primarily capitalism versus socialism), but the concept has evolved and now carries a far different nuance.

For intuitive and creative types, finding the Third Way can be more an art than a science. But it's also reachable with pure reason.

Discovering it depends almost as much on will as thought. Where others have stopped, you continue searching. There's *always* another way—and if there doesn't seem to be one, you create it. It may involve a factor or resource that wasn't immediately apparent. It may be a solution that previously wasn't possible but is now. It may come from the most unexpected of sources, in the most unexpected of ways. That's one reason it works for entrepreneurs: They've got the balls to let go and soar to the cognitive territories that would make a corporate drone airsick.

Like so many things, practice makes perfect—or at least more perfect. And after a while, searching for the Third Way starts to become second nature; it almost seems fun. That's when you start to create a game plan for every crisis that might occur and envision every possibility that might be present. It becomes almost a hobby.

That's the mentality it takes to stay cool as an entrepreneur. The mentality says: "Screw the crisis. Bring it on. I've seen it all."

IMAGINE, WHAT IF?

NOTHING HITS YOU IN THE GUT QUITE AS HARD as pouring out your heart in a presentation designed to excite people about new possibilities, and then getting blank stares or someone explicitly saying, "I don't get it."

What's that about?

In my book, it comes from a lack of imagination—and, even more specifically, from a lack of curiosity. If people are curious, they'll find a way to imagine it.

Curiosity is the root of all ambition. Curiosity is wondering: "What if I can do something that will change my life? What if I could change the world?"

That leads you naturally to the next question: "How do I do it?"

There's nothing more powerful for igniting the human spirit than curiosity. The power of curiosity supersedes even the force of the most primal emotions, because it exists at a higher plane than emotion. It's a state of mind that melds emotion and rationality into a transcendent state of mind that's full of wonder.

Too many people, though, just aren't capable of wonder. They

see what exists, and they know that there are things that *could*
exist but don't. And it means nothing to them.

I've also known people who look at the same problem or idea for years and years, and there's something about it that always keeps them curious. Then serendipity strikes, and they suddenly see something new. A better way. The Third Way.

Sometimes that's called a stroke of genius. It seems almost to arrive on wings of its own, in the same sense of genius recognized by early Greco-Roman culture: genius as coming from a genie—a magical external (not internal) force that confers special, transitory powers. But the truly magical force is not some genie. It's the power of curiosity.

Curiosity triggered the most profound change in my life. It happened during a moment when I wasn't even trying to think of a business idea or to create anything. I saw people who were playing games on their devices become visibly annoyed when ads popped up, and I wondered: "What if there was a form of advertising that people like?"

Curiosity seeks further curiosity (just as money seeks money), so I wondered: "What kind of advertising would that be?"

Funny ads? That's been done—and they're only funny the first few times. Scary ads? Fear gets attention—but nobody likes it. Happy ads? They get old as fast as funny ads. Catchy ads you just can't forget? If it's an ad, people will find a way to forget it.

The question piqued my curiosity. It left a bug in my ear.

If you get curious enough, the rest will take care of itself.

For me, curiosity was the spark that created Kiip.

Now I can share that initial spark of curiosity to drive our customers to believe in our vision as much as I do.

I go to a sales presentation and leave a bug in somebody's ear with simple little questions, like: "Why is everybody rejecting your advertising? What would it be like if you ran something that people actually responded to? What would that kind of advertising look like?"

And they're like: "Well, Brian, what *would* it look like?"

I tell them: "Think beyond the ad. It isn't even an ad; it's a reward." If the ad was the format that was leaving zero impression with consumers, it was natural that the future of advertising would have to be something entirely different.

That line piques their curiosity every time.

ABOUT THE AUTHOR

Brian Wong is the cofounder and CEO of Kiip, a leading mobile advertising network that uses innovative reward systems to redefine how brands connect with consumers. Brian received his bachelor's degree from the University of British Columbia at age eighteen after skipping four grades, and shortly after, at the age of nineteen, became one of the youngest people to ever receive venture capital funding. He has been recognized with many awards for his creative and entrepreneurial achievements, including *Forbes*'s 30 Under 30 three times, *Business Insider*'s Top 25 Under 25 in Silicon Valley, *Mashable*'s Top 5 Entrepreneurs to Watch, and the *Ad Age* Creativity Top 50. He speaks routinely to corporations such as Kraft Foods, Procter & Gamble, Unilever, L'Oréal, MasterCard, Pepsi, and Deloitte and has keynoted at SXSW, Cannes Lions, CES, *Forbes* Summits, TEDx events around the world, and more.

Kiip is reinventing how brands connect with consumers through mobile rewards. Kiip powers rewards in more than 4,000 apps on iOS and Android and works with more than 700 top brands in the world. The company has raised over $24 million in venture capital from American Express Ventures, Verizon Ventures, Relay Ventures, True Ventures, and Hummer Winblad Venture Partners and has been named one of the world's 50 Most Innovative Companies by *Fast Company*.